The

MARIE KONDO
Tidying Companion

The
MARIE KONDO
Tidying Companion

A Planner to Spark Joy
and Organize Your Life

Translated from the Japanese by Rieko Yamanaka

First published in Japan in 2018 by Fusoha Publishing Inc,
Tokyo under the title *Konmari No Mainichi Ga Tokimeku
Mahou No Katazuke*
Illustrations by Hiroko Yano

This edition first published in the UK 2023
by Bluebird, an imprint of Pan Macmillan
The Smithson, 6 Briset Street, London EC1M 5NR

EU representative: Macmillan Publishers Ireland Ltd,
1st Floor, The Liffey Trust Centre,
117–126 Sheriff Street Upper, Dublin 1, D01 YC43
Associated companies throughout the world
www.panmacmillan.com

ISBN 978-1-5290-7598-4

9 8 7 6 5 4 3 2 1

A CIP catalogue record for this book is available from the British Library.

Printed and bound in the UK by Bell and Bain Ltd, Glasgow

Visit **www.panmacmillan.com** to read more about all our books and
to buy them. You will also find features, author interviews and news of
any author events, and you can sign up for e-newsletters so that you're
always first to hear about our new releases.

Contents

Introduction

Hello, I'm Marie Kondo, a.k.a. KonMari.

The purpose of this workbook is to help you finish tidying once and for all so that you can start living a life that sparks joy. Some of you may already be familiar with the KonMari Method of tidying, but if you've found yourself hitting some kind of stumbling block or procrastinating for months, this is the perfect companion for you!

Above all else, this workbook is designed to guide you from within. In each section, I give you a breakdown of my tidying method, followed by prompts to write down your thoughts and feelings before putting what you learned into action. This helps you understand your own habits around managing possessions and weaknesses that hold you back when tidying. And self-awareness is the key to successful tidying. It's only when you uncover your true values that you can finish tidying without ever reverting to clutter again.

This workbook also has plenty of space for you to journal about your dream lifestyle as well as any observation or inner shift that you may come across over the course of the tidying process. And it's very important that you use your own hand to write them down.

These days more and more people are typing notes on their smartphone or computer, but we shouldn't underestimate the power of writing things by hand. By using our own handwriting to put our thoughts and circumstances into words, we can see ourselves much more clearly than by merely thinking in our heads.

For example, I make it a habit to carry a memo pad to jot down my thoughts and keep track of events that sparked joy. Being in frequent touch with joy in this way helps us attune to who we are and what activities or objects bring a sense of comfort or fulfillment to our lives.

Tidying is an incredible opportunity to go through this process of self-discovery in an intensive way. Let this workbook facilitate your inner dialogue as you tidy, so that you can create a clean, organized home and an ideal lifestyle that brings you joy. And if it sounds too overwhelming, don't worry – I'll walk you through the whole process step by step.

Now, grab your favourite pen and get ready to have some fun as you turn the pages!

It's not your fault that you can't tidy

You long to live in a clean and tidy home. But you have no time, no motivation, or no idea where to start. Even when you manage to tidy, clutter creeps back in sooner or later. You feel like a failure and wonder what's wrong with you. Sound familiar? Well, let me assure you: it's never your fault that you can't tidy. If you think it's because you're too busy or just not cut out for tidying, that's simply not true. The only reason why you can't tidy is that you haven't made your feelings towards your possessions clear. You're trying to store everything you have or throw things away haphazardly – without having a dialogue with them first.

The actions involved in tidying are actually quite simple. Discard things, then decide where to store what you've kept. That's it! So unless you address the root cause – your thoughts and emotions underlying the half-hearted tidying attempts and the struggle to pare things down – you'll never be done with tidying no matter how you try to store things away. I've always said that 90 per cent of tidying is in the mind. And to adopt the right mindset, you need to first become aware of how you really feel. Tuning in to what sparks joy will make your tidying process so much easier as you go through your belongings and recognize how you feel towards each one.

You only need to do two things in tidying

Discard
= Keep only what really sparks joy

Designate storage
= Focus on joy as you put things away

How this workbook helps you master tidying

1. Make progress effortlessly

You can't succeed in tidying unless you change your mindset first. And for the process to go smoothly, it's important to follow the steps in order. With this workbook, even if you have no clue where to start, all you need to do is follow my prompts on each page. As you write down your response, you'll become aware of your feelings towards your belongings and understand what action you need to take in that moment.

2. Develop your sensitivity to joy

In my one-on-one tidying lessons, I walk my clients through the process of taking each object by hand and asking themselves if it sparks joy. Since joy is not something we normally pay much attention to, it can be difficult to cultivate the awareness for it without guidance. The beauty of this workbook is that, as you repeatedly write down your thoughts and feelings, you'll become increasingly aware of what brings you joy. It can be as effective as taking an actual private lesson with me!

Go at your own pace

It's up to you how much time you want
to spend on tidying. Ideally you would
complete it in one shot during a short
period of time, but if that's not possible,
feel free to go at your own pace. Tidy
on your days off, or a few hours each
day. That way, you won't give up
halfway. A realistic timeframe is
another key to success.

The basic rules of the KonMari Method

RULE 1

Tidy by category, not by location

Many people suffer from relapse after tidying because they make the mistake of tidying by location. The problem with this approach is that you can't grasp how much you actually have. Objects in the same category are often dispersed all over the house, which makes it hard to recognize you have too many. That's why tidying by category is a must. When tidying books, for example, start by gathering all the books and magazines around the house in one place. This way, you can immediately see the total volume and realize how much stuff you've kept that isn't even necessary. It's this revelation that propels you to the next step.

RULE 2

Tidy in the correct order

The first category to sort through is your clothes. Since you wear them every day, it's relatively easy to do your 'joy check' on them, and they make good practice for developing an awareness of joy. From there, as you move on to books, papers, komono (miscellany), and finally sentimental items, your sensitivity to joy will gradually increase.

Clothes ⇨ Books ⇨ Papers ⇨ Komono (miscellany) ⇨ Sentimental items

RULE 3

Clarify your intention before tidying

Always tidy your own belongings first

It's tempting to tidy your family members' belongings along with your own, but remember everyone has different values towards objects. It's not for us to judge what's necessary and what isn't for others. Always start by tidying your own things.

The key to tidying is your own mindset and feelings towards your lifestyle, so it's crucial to make them clear for yourself. Using the worksheets to write down your thoughts and observations at each step will help you make tangible progress in your tidying.

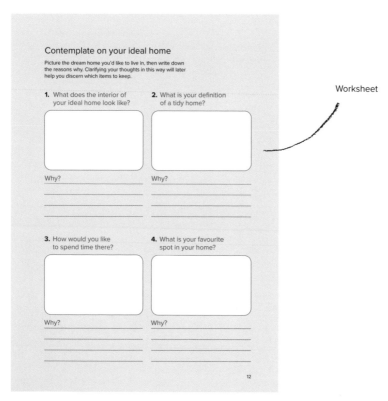

Worksheet

Contemplate on your ideal home

Picture the dream home you'd like to live in, then write down the reasons why. Clarifying your thoughts in this way will later help you discern which items to keep.

1. What does the interior of your ideal home look like?

Why?

2. What is your definition of a tidy home?

Why?

3. How would you like to spend time there?

Why?

4. What is your favourite spot in your home?

Why?

12

Your roadmap to successful tidying

Perhaps you dread tidying, or you've read my books but haven't been able to take the first step. Maybe your tidying attempts so far have ended in disaster. Whatever the case, please know that I designed this workbook to help you succeed in tidying.

Anyone can tidy. If done properly, you won't relapse into clutter, either. The only reason why you get tripped up is because you're not approaching it correctly. Following the steps in proper order is essential if you want to tidy smoothly. In this workbook I provide step-by-step instructions on how to succeed in your tidying marathon, so that you'll never get lost. First, visualize your ideal home and lifestyle vividly. Next, go through each category (clothes, books, papers, komono and sentimental items, in that order), gathering all corresponding items in one spot. Touch each item in your pile and keep only what sparks joy. Lastly, think about where in your home each remaining item belongs and store it properly. That's the overall flow. At each step, there'll be worksheets for writing down observations and thoughts that help you stay present with yourself throughout the process, instead of getting overwhelmed by the tasks and leaving your heart behind. By the time you've completed the entire workbook, you'll be living in a space that brings utmost joy to you, filled only with your favourite objects that are neatly put away.

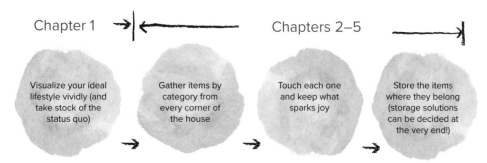

Chapter 1 → | ← —————— →   Chapters 2–5   —————— →|

Visualize your ideal lifestyle vividly (and take stock of the status quo)

→

Gather items by category from every corner of the house

→

Touch each one and keep what sparks joy

→

Store the items where they belong (storage solutions can be decided at the very end!)

Choose what to keep based on joy

When tidying, it's essential to finish discarding first. You may find it difficult to throw anything away without a good reason, but that's a sign that you're caught up in choosing what to throw away. Instead, focus on choosing what to keep. And how do we do that? By tuning in to joy. It may sound too vague, but the whole purpose of tidying is to bring you happiness, so it's important that you choose and keep what makes you happy.

The key to discerning whether something sparks joy is to take each item in your hand and actually touch it. How does it feel against your skin? Is it something you'd like to keep around? Take a moment to feel the reaction in your body. If you sense an uplifting energy, it's definitely a keeper. If the item doesn't speak to your heart, however, it's time to let it go. When saying goodbye to an object, it's important to express gratitude for its service. For example, if it's a piece of expensive clothing that you never wore, you can say to it, 'Thank you for teaching me what kind of clothes don't suit me.' By acknowledging the purpose it fulfilled and giving thanks, you can feel less guilty about throwing it away. You can also donate it to charity or sell it, of course.

What if you can't tell what sparks joy?

• Be patient with yourself
• Pick out your top three favourites by intuition
• Give the object a big hug

Understanding what it feels like for something to spark joy can be difficult at first – and that's okay. Try comparing items within the same category. You can even rank them in order – pick out your top three outfits, for example. Another helpful trick is to not only touch the object but to give it a big hug.

Chapter 1

Before you start tidying

If you're eager to dive straight into tidying, hold your horses! There are a couple of things you still need to do before getting started. First of all, are you mentally prepared? Make a commitment right now to tidy with all your heart so that your life sparks joy. Then it's time to journal about the ideal lifestyle you dream of.

Visualize your ideal home

Before you start tidying, take some time to imagine your ideal home and describe it in writing. This is not the time to play small! Browse through home interior magazines and websites, let your fantasies run wild, and dream as big as you can. Once you have the basic idea, visualize it vividly and with as much detail as you can. What does the décor look like, and what draws you to that style? How would you spend time there, and why? As you inquire deeper, the vision for your happiness will begin to take shape. Seeing a clear destination for your tidying journey makes a huge difference in your motivation.

Completed worksheet example

Freely describe your ideal home. Don't worry about whether it's realistic or not. Verbalizing your vision of a house or room that truly sparks joy is the fast track to successful tidying.

For each response, ask yourself why you think that way. This gives you more clarity and helps you shape a concrete vision of your happiness.

Contemplate on your ideal home

Picture the dream home you'd like to live in, then write down the reasons why. Clarifying your thoughts in this way will later help you discern which items to keep.

1. What does the interior of your ideal home look like?

Why?

2. What is your definition of a tidy home?

Why?

3. How would you like to spend time there?

Why?

4. What is your favourite spot in your home?

Why?

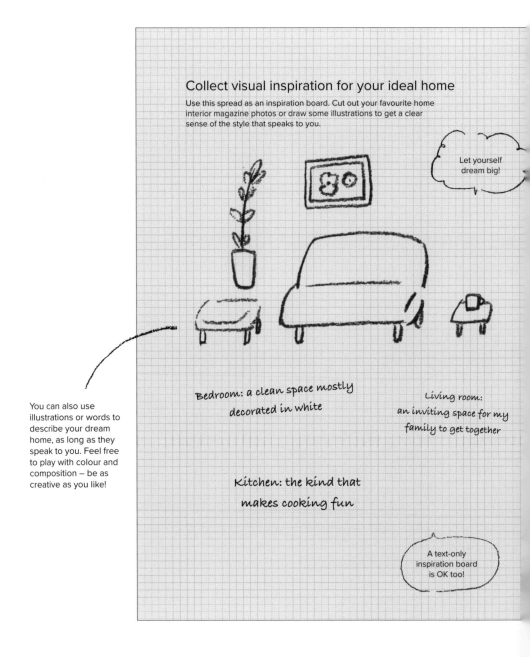

Collect visual inspiration for your ideal home

Use this spread as an inspiration board. Cut out your favourite home interior magazine photos or draw some illustrations to get a clear sense of the style that speaks to you.

Let yourself dream big!

Bedroom: a clean space mostly decorated in white

Living room: an inviting space for my family to get together

Kitchen: the kind that makes cooking fun

A text-only inspiration board is OK too!

You can also use illustrations or words to describe your dream home, as long as they speak to you. Feel free to play with colour and composition – be as creative as you like!

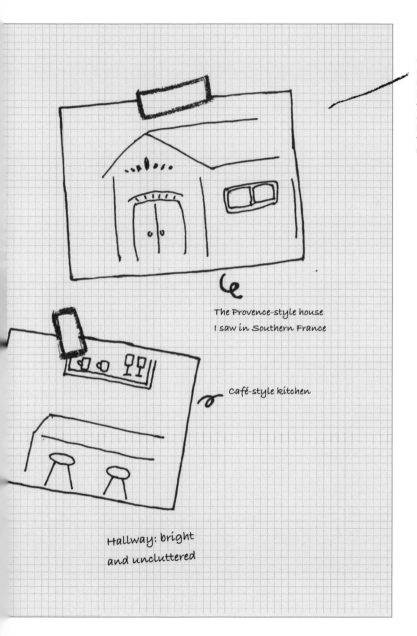

Cut out and paste magazine photos of houses and home interiors that inspire you, perhaps from a foreign country. Pictures are a great tool for boosting motivation!

The Provence-style house
I saw in Southern France

Café-style kitchen

Hallway: bright
and uncluttered

Collect visual inspiration for your ideal home

Use this spread as an inspiration board. Cut out your favourite home interior magazine photos or draw some illustrations to get a clear sense of the style that speaks to you.

Let yourself dream big!

A text-only inspiration board is OK too!

Design your ideal lifestyle

Your ideal morning

How would you like to spend time at home after you wake up in the morning? Write down your ideal schedule. List specific activities, such as 'enjoy a cup of tea' or 'vacuum my room', so that you can form a clear picture in your mind. Then think about what state your home needs to be in to make that possible. As you'll soon discover, tidying is an absolute prerequisite for you to spend time in a productive and fulfilling way.

Completed worksheet example

Write down what you need to do, with regard to tidying, in order to make your ideal behaviour possible. For example, if you want to do stretching exercises, you would need the floor to be clean and tidy.

A moment of joy in the morning sets the tone for the day. The more detailed you are in describing your vision, the more likely it is that it will become reality.

'Morning time' is until you leave the house to go to work or school. If you're a homemaker or working from home, break up your day by deciding that your morning ends at, say, 9 a.m.

Your ideal morning routine

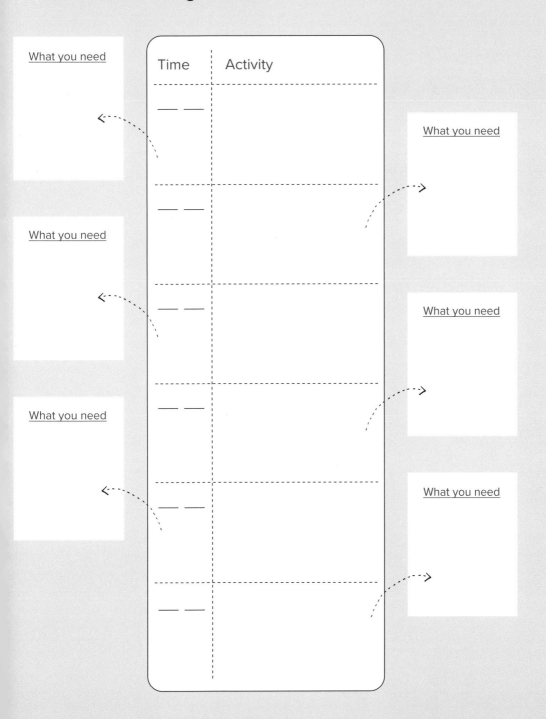

Time	Activity
— —	
— —	
— —	
— —	
— —	
— —	

What you need

What you need

What you need

What you need

What you need

What you need

Your ideal evening routine

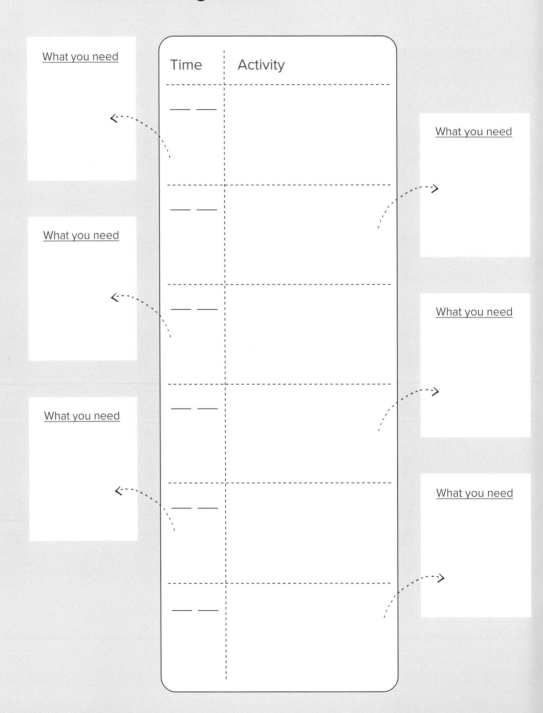

Time	Activity
— — —	
— — —	
— —	
— — —	
— —	
— — —	

What you need

What you need

What you need

What you need

What you need

What you need

Your ideal evening

Now that you've designed your ideal morning routine, do the same for your evenings – from the moment you leave work or school, get groceries for dinner, and after you come home. The way you spend time before bed affects the quality of your sleep and how you feel when you wake up the following morning. So think about how you can rearrange your home and lifestyle to facilitate a good night's sleep. It's all about relaxation, so be sure to avoid stimulation and carve out some time and space to help you wind down.

Completed worksheet example

What kind of a space would you find relaxing? Perhaps it's one with a dining table that's clean and clear. Visualizing in this way helps to clarify what you need for your ideal evening time.

Picture yourself spending time after coming home, for a pleasant night's sleep in preparation for another day. Don't try to cram too many things in.

Just before going to bed, take a moment to express gratitude for the day, your home and belongings, and the people around you. This clears the mind, helping you wake up refreshed in the morning.

Things to avoid before bedtime

Screen time

Staring at the bright screen of a smartphone or computer monitor is stressful to the eyes and brain. I do my best to avoid them late at night so that my sleep doesn't get compromised.

Cold drinks

Drinking cold beverages activates the sympathetic nervous system and weakens the functions of the parasympathetic nervous system, which you need for sleep. So before bedtime I stick to soothing, hot beverages with no caffeine.

Observe the current state of your home

Once you have a clear vision for your destination, it's time to take stock of the shape of your home. The key here is to take inventory of all the storage spaces around the home. Knowing what storage is available will make it easier for you to decide where to put things later. Plus, if you go around your home taking photos of the rooms and storage spaces, you can see the current level of clutter. These 'before' photos are sure to get you excited about the changes tidying can bring.

Completed worksheet example

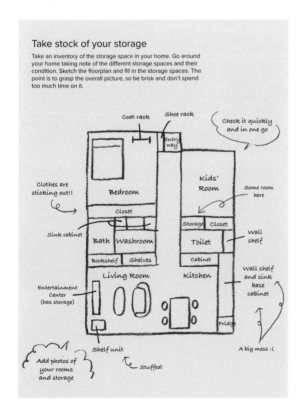

Go around your home and sketch a rough floorplan. Add quick notes about what kind of storage spaces you have (cupboards, shelves, etc.) and where they are located.

Don't worry about what's currently occupying the storage spaces. Just be sure to check and make note of the level of fullness: 'completely stuffed', 'plenty of room here', etc.

Take stock of your storage

Take an inventory of the storage space in your home. Go around your home taking note of the different storage spaces and their condition. Sketch the floorplan and fill in the storage spaces. The point is to grasp the overall picture, so be brisk and don't spend too much time on it.

Completed worksheet example

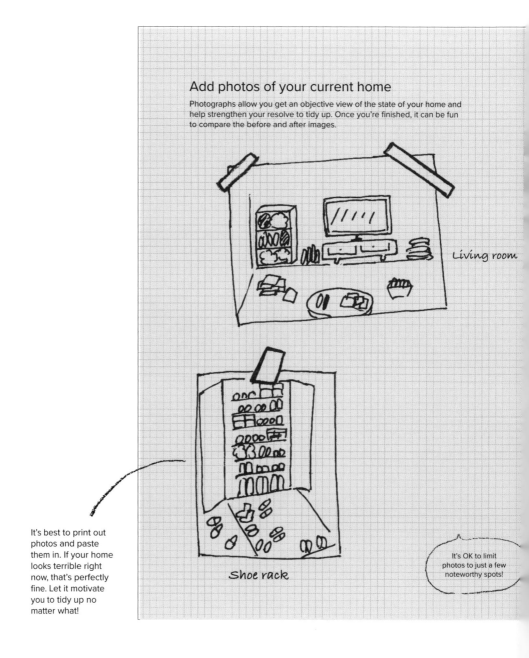

Add photos of your current home

Photographs allow you get an objective view of the state of your home and help strengthen your resolve to tidy up. Once you're finished, it can be fun to compare the before and after images.

Living room

Shoe rack

It's best to print out photos and paste them in. If your home looks terrible right now, that's perfectly fine. Let it motivate you to tidy up no matter what!

It's OK to limit photos to just a few noteworthy spots!

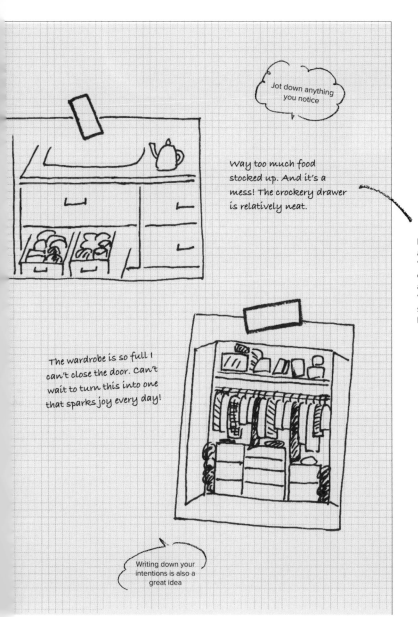

Feel free to jot down anything that you notice: 'Things in the same category are scattered around the house', 'The wardrobe looks suffocated', 'The bathroom looks pretty good', etc.

33

Add photos of your current home

Photographs allow you get an objective view of the state of your home and help strengthen your resolve to tidy up. Once you're finished, it can be fun to compare the before and after images.

It's OK to limit photos to just a few noteworthy spots!

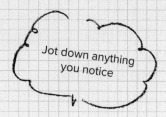

Jot down anything you notice

Writing down your intentions is also a great idea

Set the tidying timeline

I think of tidying as a special event: something to get done in a brief period, instead of aimlessly working on it forever. So decide now when you're going to start and finish. Once you're done with the 'tidying festival', all you need to do on a daily basis is put things back in their designated storage after you use them. With no more need to wrestle with tidying, you'll be free to live peacefully in a space that you love. When you think of it that way, doesn't tidying seem more and more like a fun event?

It's up to you how much time you want to spend tidying. The point is to timebox something that you may otherwise drag your feet on.

You can change the end date at any time

Once you start tidying, you may find that it takes more time than you thought. But don't give up! You can change the end date at any point. The idea is to have a set due date at all times. If you have a lot of stuff or are short on time, feel free to set the end date for just one category at a time (clothing, for example).

Set your goal

Clothes	Start on _____(month) _____(day) at _____(time) Finish by _____(month) _____(day) at _____(time)
Books	Start on _____(month) _____(day) at _____(time) Finish by _____(month) _____(day) at _____(time)
Papers	Start on _____(month) _____(day) at _____(time) Finish by _____(month) _____(day) at _____(time)
Komono	Start on _____(month) _____(day) at _____(time) Finish by _____(month) _____(day) at _____(time)
Sentimental items	Start on _____(month) _____(day) at _____(time) Finish by _____(month) _____(day) at _____(time)

I will finish tidying everything by

_____ (year)

_____ (month) _____ (day)

Tidying timeline examples

Here are some client testimonials from my private tidying lessons. Find someone you can relate to and use their case study as a reference point for setting your own tidying timeline.

The busy and overwhelmed 'little by little' type

T, a working mum in her thirties, took eight months

I live in a five-bedroom house with my family of five. Because the house is too big for its own sake, it was filled with so much stuff. At first I had a hard time letting things go. I did one lesson per month. After going through the kitchen komono at around lesson #5, my house started to feel nice and uncluttered. That's when my family members started to tidy with me. A total of eight lessons in eight months transformed both my house and family!

I, a woman in her forties with a super-demanding full-time job, took a year and a half

I live by myself in a two-bedroom flat. I had a ton of clothes – during the first session, I went through them for eight hours straight, and in the second one I worked on the accessories. My pace was one lesson every few months, and I finished tidying my whole flat after a total of six. Looking back, I could have taken some time off work to get it done more quickly, but I'm happy that it went a lot more smoothly than trying to tackle it on my own.

The quick and focused 'intensive' type

Y, a homemaker in her forties who moves frequently due to her husband's work, took two weeks

I live in a two-bedroom flat with my family of three. I decided to sign up for tidying sessions when I found out we'd be moving in a month because of my husband's job. I tidied in four lessons over two weeks: clothes, books and papers in the first lesson, komono in the second and third, and sentimental items in the fourth. I was able to let go of so much, including clothes that my child had outgrown, dishes I never used, and mountains of paper. And as an added bonus, downsizing helped us keep our moving cost down!

K, a woman in her thirties with a full-time job, took a month and a half

I live alone in a one-bedroom flat. I finished tidying in four lessons over a month and a half: clothes in the first lesson, books and papers in the second, komono (except kitchen-related ones) in the third, and kitchen komono and sentimental items in the fourth. I also worked on tidying thoroughly in between lessons, so I was able to make consistent progress in a short period, which helped me build self-confidence in the end.

You're now ready to tidy!

Now that you have envisioned your ideal lifestyle and taken an inventory of your home, it's time to start tidying! Take a moment to write down your intentions and current state of mind so that you can look back on them as many times as you like along the way.

1. Once again, what is the lifestyle you dream of?

2. How are you feeling right now?

3. What are your intentions?

Be even more
specific than the first
time around

Chapter 2

Tidy your clothes

Your tidying campaign begins with clothes. It's a simple category in that it's relatively easy to decide whether to keep or discard each item, which makes it the perfect place to start. As you pick out the clothes you love from a vast number of options and journal about the experience along the way, you will become more and more sensitive to what brings you joy. Plus, we will go over the KonMari Method of folding and storing clothes.

Fill in the dates when you started and finished

Started _____ (year) _____ (month)

_____ (day) at _____ (time)

Finished _____ (year) _____ (month)

_____ (day) at _____ (time)

How to tidy without relapsing

Tidying clothes consists of four steps: gather all your clothes from every corner of the house, choose what sparks joy, fold them, then store them. Bags and shoes are also included in this category.

1. Gather

Gather all your clothes from every corner of the house

Go through your entire house picking up every single piece of clothing you have and pile them up in one spot. Most of you will be shocked by the sheer volume. It's important to write this reaction down in the worksheet, so that you can grasp the amount of stuff you have. Now let's climb this mountain of clothes!

They're everywhere!

The 'joy check' order

The closer to the heart an item is worn, the easier it is to tell if it sparks joy. For efficiency, start with tops, then go in the order given here. Tidying one subcategory at a time is especially useful for when you have a particularly large amount or don't have the luxury of carving out big chunks of time.

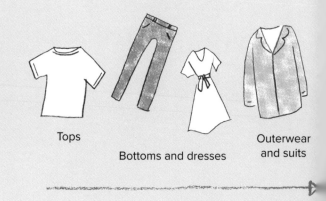

Tops

Bottoms and dresses

Outerwear and suits

2. Keep what sparks joy

Touch each piece and keep only what sparks joy

One by one, take a piece from the clothing pile and ask yourself if it sparks joy. Don't try to keep something because it's still new or can be turned into loungewear. Choose only what your heart says yes to! Once you've gone through the whole pile, you may be left with a third or a quarter of what you started out with.

Doesn't spark joy   Sparks joy 💜

Socks

Underwear

Bags

Clothing accessories

Clothes for specific events

Shoes

3. Fold

Fold as many clothes as you can

Clothing storage involves either folding or hanging – and folding is the more efficient use of space by far. It's also a way of transmitting energy to the clothes through your hands. So unless it's a coat or other bulky item that takes up less space when hung, go ahead and fold everything you can.

Your wardrobe will only have clothes that you love!

4. Store

Put away the clothes on hangers first, then folded clothes second

When storing clothes, start with the ones you put on hangers. Hang taller items on the left and shorter ones on the right. This creates a line that slopes up to the right, which feels naturally pleasing. If you realize that some of the clothes you put on hangers can actually be folded, take them off and fold them. Then store all of the folded clothes.

Tops

Tops such as tees, blouses and sweaters are relatively easy to do joy checks on. Gather them and write down anything you've noticed. Then go through the pile, choose what sparks joy, and fold them. As for the items that didn't make the cut, express gratitude for their service before letting them go.

Gather all items in one pile and write down your observations

Example:
- Lots of black tops
- 60 T-shirts total
- Some clothes were in a worse shape than I thought

For your own shopping reference

Touch each one and keep only what sparks joy

If you're having trouble deciding, it's helpful to start with the off-season tops. Since you won't be wearing them right away, it's easier to tell whether they bring you joy. When in doubt, ask yourself these questions:

Helpful questions for difficult joy checks

- When was the last time I wore this?
- Would I want to see this again next season?
- Am I willing to take good care of it?
- Do I feel good about myself when I wear it?

Give thanks to what doesn't spark joy and let it go

Give a rough estimate, e.g. 'two bin bags full' or '30 pieces'

Fold what you can so it can be stored upright

The first step in folding clothes is to make a long rectangle. Then you turn it into a smaller rectangle that stands up on its own. When clothes are folded properly, they stand up. Until you get the hang of it, keep making adjustments until they do – and you will become a master at it eventually.

Basic method: how to fold short-sleeved tops

Smooth out the wrinkles with your hands

Make a long rectangle

1. Spread the shirt facing up. Fold one third of the shirt across the centre

2. Fold the sleeve back over the folded third so that it doesn't stick out.

3. Fold the other side the same way, forming a rectangle.

This gap here is key
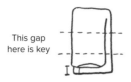

Done!

4. Fold the rectangle in half from the collar towards the hem. Leave a bit of gap at the hem for a clean finish.

5. Pick up the previous fold and fold two or three more times towards the hem, making a small rectangle.

6. Check to see if it stands on its own while holding its shape. If it doesn't, adjust the width or the number of folds.

How to fold long-sleeved tops

Smooth out wrinkles
as you go

1. As with the basic method for folding short-sleeved tops, fold one third of the shirt towards the centre.

2. Fold the sleeve back so that it doesn't overlap the opposite third.

3. Fold the sleeve downwards so that it aligns with the body of the garment.

Make sure the sleeves
don't overlap

Done!

4. Fold the other side the same way, forming a rectangle.

5. Fold the rectangle in half from the collar towards the hem. Then pick up the fold you just created and fold two or three more times towards the hem.

6. If the compact rectangle stands on its own, you're finished. Garments made of flimsy materials need not stand up.

Bottoms and dresses

Next, go through bottoms and dresses. It's helpful to do this by category: skirts, trousers, jeans and so on. If there's an item you're planning to wear once you lose weight, visualize yourself working hard towards that goal, then ask yourself if it sparks joy. If all you feel is a sense of attachment, then it's time to let it go.

Does it flatter your current body type? Is it on trend?

Gather all items in one pile and write down your observations

Example:
- 15 pairs of jeans
- Found a pair of trousers that didn't fit
- A lot of the skirts look the same

Touch each one and keep only what sparks joy

If you love trousers, go through the skirts first, and vice versa. It's easier to start with things that you're less attached to. Bottoms support your lower body, so keep only what truly sparks joy.

Downgrading to loungewear is taboo

Many people like to take the clothes that didn't make the cut and turn them into 'loungewear' – and they never wear them. All they're doing is holding off on letting it go. If you want loungewear, get some that you actually love instead.

Give thanks to what doesn't spark joy and let it go

Give a rough estimate, e.g. 'two bin bags full' or '30 pieces'

Fold what you can so it can be stored upright

The basic idea for folding trousers and skirts is the same as tops: make a long rectangle first. Generally speaking, bottoms made of denim, cotton or wool can be folded. Pleated trousers, skirts that wrinkle and dresses, on the other hand, are better stored on a hanger.

Basic method: how to fold trousers

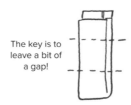

The key is to leave a bit of a gap!

1. Fold the trousers in half lengthways over the front. If the seat sticks out, fold it against the trouser leg.

2. Fold in half from the hem to the waistband, leaving a gap before it for a clean finish.

Done!

3. Fold in thirds.

4. If the small rectangle stands on its own, you're finished. Adjust the number of folds according to the length of the trouser legs.

How to fold skirts

1. Spread the skirt facing up, and fold one third lengthways towards the centre.

2. Fold the skirt back so that it doesn't overlap the opposite third.

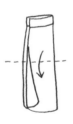

3. Fold the other side in the same way, forming a rectangle. Fold in half from the waistband towards the hem, leaving a gap at the end.

Long skirts can be rolled up

4. Fold two or three times from the previous fold to the hem, making a small rectangle.

How to fold dresses

1. Spread the dress facing up, then fold one third lengthways towards the centre.

2. Fold the sleeve and skirt back so that they don't overlap the opposite third. For flared skirts, fold any protruding part back against the first fold.

Like folding origami

3. Fold the other side in the same way, forming a rectangle.

4. Fold in half from the collar to the hem. Then fold two or three more times.

5. If the small rectangle stands up on its own, you're finished.

Outerwear and suits

As a rule of thumb, store jackets, suits and coats on hangers. Once you've picked out the ones that spark joy, keep them in a separate pile with the hangers still on. Some outerwear such as knitted coats and down jackets can be folded, so you may opt to store them that way during the off-seasons.

Are you holding on to a coat just because it was pricey?

Gather all items in one pile and write down your observations

Example:
• One coat had a hole in it
• One suit was outdated
• There were three jackets I hadn't worn in years!

Set aside the clothes that look like they don't want to be folded

As you go through your clothes, keep the ones you had on hangers in a separate pile. If you've been storing almost all of your clothes on hangers, however, do fold everything except the pieces that look like they'd rather not be folded.

Touch each one and keep only what sparks joy

It can be daunting to let go of coats and suits that cost a lot of money. To counter this, try them on and look at yourself in the mirror. You'll be able to tell the difference right away, and the decision will make itself.

Give thanks to what doesn't spark joy and let it go

Give a rough estimate, e.g. 'two bin bags full' or '30 pieces'

Fold what you can – a little loosely

Knitted coats and down jackets are made of thick materials and contain a lot of air, so fold them a bit more loosely than usual. If it's very bulky and takes up too much space, I recommend you put it in a reusable shopping bag or drawstring bag and push the air out before storing it.

How to fold a knitted coat

1. Spread the coat facing up, and fold in half lengthways.

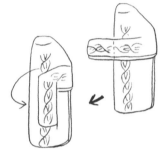

2. Stack the sleeves, and fold them first in the opposite direction. Then fold them downwards so that they're flush with the length of the coat. You now have a long rectangle.

Adjust based on length and thickness

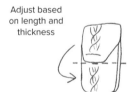

3. Depending on the length of the coat, fold in thirds or quarters from the collar to the hem.

Done!

4. Once you have a small rectangle, you're finished. Since it contains a lot of air, it doesn't have to stand up.

How to fold a down jacket

1. Spread the jacket facing up, and fold in half lengthways. Stack the sleeves and fold them downwards, forming a rectangle.

2. Depending on the length, fold in half or thirds from the collar to the hem. You may choose to store this rectangle in the drawer as it is.

Really squeeze the air out

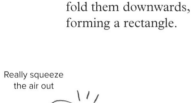

Done!

3. If you want to make it even more compact, press on the jacket to deflate it as you slip it into a cloth shopping bag or a drawstring bag about two sizes smaller.

4. Store the bag sideways. If you don't have a bag, you can also wrap it in a furoshiki (traditional square Japanese wrapping cloth) or a large scarf.

Socks, tights and leggings

If you have a large amount, go through them by category: socks, tights, stockings, leggings and so on. Don't forget to include tights still in their packages and anything else you've been stockpiling. Once you've finished selecting, fold them carefully. Never ball them up or tie them in a knot. Store them in a comfortable state so that they can enjoy a good rest, even for a little while.

Gather all items in one pile and write down your observations

Example:
• There were a lot of extra tights
• A few socks were missing their pair

_____

_____

_____

_____

_____

Touch each one and keep only what sparks joy

We tend to hold on to socks without giving them much thought, so prioritize the pairs that evoke positive emotions, such as making you feel put together or giving you motivation at work.

Give thanks to what doesn't spark joy and let it go

Give a rough estimate, e.g. 'One shopping bag full, 20 pairs of socks', etc.

Fold your items carefully

How to fold socks

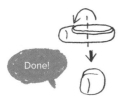

Short socks

Low-cut socks for flats and trainers can be stacked and folded in half.

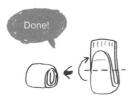

Regular socks

As for regular crew-length socks, stack the pair and fold them in half to form a rectangle. Fold this two or three more times to make a smaller rectangle.

Socks that support your lifestyle pass the joy test

Work- or school-related tights or socks may not seem that exciting, but if they support your lifestyle, consider them as bringing you joy. Be sure to keep only the ones that are in good condition.

How to fold tights

1. Fold one leg over the other with the front facing in.

2. Fold in thirds from the toes towards the waistband.

3. Roll up the rectangle from the fold towards the waistband.

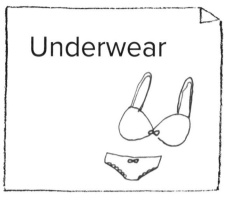

Underwear

Gather all items in one pile and write down your observations

Example:
• Lots of underwear is looking shabby
• Haven't replaced my bras in years

_____

_____

_____

_____

This category includes not only bras and pants but also bra tops, shapewear, slips, vests, and anything you wear as base layer for warmth. In particular, I consider bras royalty and treat them with extra respect. Be sure to keep only the ones that make you sparkle, and fold them in a way that delights you as well.

Touch each one and keep only what sparks joy

Don't compromise on underwear, especially because it comes into direct contact with your skin. A helpful question to ask is whether you feel good about yourself when you wear it.

Give thanks to what doesn't spark joy and let it go

Give a rough estimate, e.g. 'One bra, three pairs of pants', etc.

Carefully fold what you can

How to fold bras

Treat them like royalty

1. Turn the bra over and tuck the straps and bands into the cups.

Done!

2. Turn it over to the front and make sure the cups aren't flattened.

Keep functional underwear based on whether it improves the quality of your life

For purely functional pieces such as base layers, let the focus of your joy check be on whether they improve the quality of your life, for example by bringing you warmth or comfort.

How to fold pants

1. Spread the pair facing down, and fold the crotch upward.

2. Fold the sides over the crotch as if to envelop it. Roll up from the bottom fold towards the waistband.

Done!

3. Turn over the roll to show any decoration on the waistband.

Bags

Are you hesitant to get rid of an old bag? A surprising number of people believe bags can't be thrown away. Unless you consciously replace them from time to time, the bags that mean the most to you will get buried in the mix before you know it. Once you know which ones to keep, fold or stack them so that they take up as little space as possible. Don't forget to include plastic and cloth shopping bags in this category as well.

Count shopping bags and tidy them impassively

We tend to stock up on shopping bags for carrying extra things. Consider how many you actually use, and make your decision with a cool head. Store them in hard containers such as a file box to prevent them from accumulating.

Gather all items in one pile and write down your observations

Example:
• I had more than 10 reusable shopping bags! They were all gifts from others
• There was mould growing on the leather bag I pulled out from the back of the wardrobe

_____

_____

_____

_____

_____

_____

_____

_____

_____

_____

Touch each one and keep only what sparks joy

If you find yourself passing on a particular bag every time you consider it, it's already served its purpose. You can tell by touching it with your hands.

Give thanks to what doesn't spark joy and let it go

Give a rough estimate, e.g. 'Five reusable shopping bags', etc.

Bag-in-bag method

Empty the bags, and pair them up by similar material, size or frequency of use. Stack one inside the other. Don't store more than two bags in one.

Fold and stack what you've chosen

Reusable shopping bags

1. Spread the bag. Stack the handles and fold them in. Fold the bag in half or thirds lengthways, depending on the width.

2. Fold in half from the opening towards the bottom. Then fold in half again.

Done!

3. Once the small rectangle stands upright, you're finished. Bags made of flimsy materials need not stand up.

Clothing accessories

This category includes scarves, wraps, belts, gloves, hats, any accessories that come with a piece of clothing and other knick-knacks that have to do with getting dressed. They tend to be scattered about, so make sure you gather them in one spot for the selection process. Once you've chosen which ones to keep, fold what you can. As for belts, roll them up to save space or hang them in the wardrobe.

'This might come in handy' is not joy

Holding on to clothing accessories 'just in case' is a no-no, whether it's a detachable fur collar that came with a coat or a ribbon that matches a skirt. If they spark joy, decide how you will use them, and if not, bid them farewell.

Gather all items in one pile and write down your observations

Example:
- So many wraps were piled up and wrinkled
- Five black belts seem too many

_____

_____

_____

_____

_____

Touch each one and keep only what sparks joy

You'll likely have an easier time starting with items that had been tucked away and out of your sight for a long time.

Give thanks to what doesn't spark joy and let it go

Give a rough estimate, e.g. 'One bin bag full, 10 accessories', etc.

Fold or roll up what you've chosen into small shapes

How to fold wraps

1. Spread the wrap and fold it in half or thirds lengthways, depending on the width.

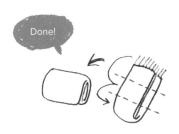

2. Fold in half widthways. If the wrap has a fringe, tuck it in, then fold it two or three times. Once you have a small rectangle, you're finished.

How to roll up belts

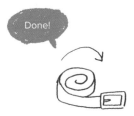

Roll the belt towards the buckle.

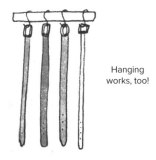

Hanging works, too!

If you have room in your wardrobe, you can also hang belts on hooks or a belt hanger. Choose whichever method suits you.

Clothes for specific events

Gather all items in one pile and write down your observations

Example:
- Can't wear the same Halloween costume two years in a row
- Still love the dress I made three years ago!

_____

_____

_____

_____

_____

_____

_____

_____

_____

_____

_____

Swimsuits, eveningwear, ski gear, holiday outfits, stage costumes . . . these are clothes you may only wear once a year, but you can of course keep them if they spark joy. If you have a particularly large number of items associated with a single activity or event (for example, you own many kimonos because you practise Japanese tea ceremony), you may want to set them aside and go through them later along with hobby komono (p.142).

How much did you let go?

Touch each one and keep only what sparks joy

Swimsuits are quick to go out of style, even if they still fit. Ask yourself if you definitely want to wear it next season.

Give thanks to what doesn't spark joy and let it go

Give a rough estimate, e.g. 'Two swimsuits, five outfits for specific events', etc.

Fold what you can so it can be stored upright

Whether it's ski gear, swimsuits, holiday outfits or dance costumes, fold it into a small rectangle, as you would any other piece of clothing.

Store them together in one container

It's best to gather and store all event-specific clothes in one large storage box, instead of separating them by type. This way, you'll never have to go looking for them. You may choose to store some of them with seasonal komono (p.157), as long as they belong to the same activity.

Wear your costumes at home

You may have clothes that you wouldn't wear outside but they still bring you joy, such as old costumes. If that's the case, why not wear them around the house? Enjoy it to your heart's content in the privacy of your own home. And if you change your mind after catching a glimpse of yourself in the mirror, that's perfectly fine, too.

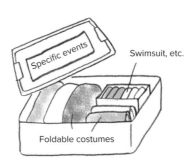

Specific events

Swimsuit, etc.

Foldable costumes

Shoes

Shoes are the last clothing category to tidy. They take up substantial space, so finish storing away all the previous categories before tackling them. Tidying shoes clears up the hallway, which is a happy side effect. With its 'face' nice and tidy, the entire home lightens up.

Gather every pair of shoes from around the house

Lay down some newspaper on the floor and gather every pair of shoes from the hallway, wardrobes and all around your house. Line them up by type (shoes, trainers, boots, etc.) to make the selection process nice and easy. Don't forget to include indoor slippers in this category.

Gather all items in one pile and write down your observations

Example:
• I'm always wearing the same pair of shoes
• There's a pair of trainers that could do with washing

_____

_____

_____

_____

_____

_____

_____

_____

_____

Touch each one and keep only what sparks joy

A pair of shoes that you love are sure to take you to wonderful places in life. When you think of it that way, which pair would you like to keep?

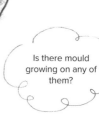

Is there mould growing on any of them?

Give thanks to what doesn't spark joy and let it go

Give a rough estimate, e.g. 'one pair of shoes, three pairs of trainers', etc.

Fold what you can so it can be stored upright

Whether it's ski gear, swimsuits, holiday outfits or dance costumes, fold it into a small rectangle, as you would any other piece of clothing. Kimonos and yukatas should be folded in the traditional way and stored flat.

Wipe down the soles of the shoes you've chosen

You may not have paid much attention to the soles of your shoes before, but they literally wear themselves out to support you. Wipe them clean with gratitude, and let your mind clear up as well.

Let go of shoes that hurt to wear, even if you love them

You'll probably never wear shoes that make your feet hurt, even if you love the design. Unless you're determined to put it on display as a piece of art, it's best to say goodbye.

Now let's store them all!

STEP 1

Hang clothes in an upward slope to the right

Now we're in the final stage: designate a location for each piece of clothing you've chosen, and store it there. I recommend storing on- and off-season clothes together, so that you have easy access to them and can grasp the exact amount of clothes you have. Begin by storing the clothes that are better hung than folded. Hang them in an upward slope to the right, keeping them sorted by category.

Gather the clothes that hang, and put them on hangers

Gather the clothes you didn't fold, such as coats and suits, and put them on hangers if you haven't already. If you're using a mishmash of hangers, switch them out with a set that has uniform colour and material to enhance the joy factor.

Presentation matters

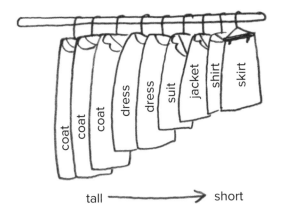

tall ──────────> short

Hang the clothes in an upward slope to the right

A line that slopes upwards to the right has a naturally uplifting effect. Hang clothes from left to right, from the longest to the shortest: coats, then dresses, suits, shirts and so on. At the same time, think about creating a gradient with the material (thickest to thinnest) and colour (darkest to lightest). Now you'll get a thrill every time you open the wardrobe!

Trouser and skirt hangers are useful, too

If you have too many clothes to hang, take another look and see if some of them can be folded instead. This creates more room in the wardrobe and saves valuable storage space.

STEP 2

Store the folded clothes according to colour

Once you've folded clothes into compact rectangle shapes, the basic rule is to store them upright in a drawer. Within each category, divide them roughly by shape or material instead of by season. Arrange them so as to create a colour gradient. Not only does this look beautiful, it also makes it easy to see where everything is and grasp the overall colour palette of your wardrobe.

Sort the tops by shape, then by texture of the material

Sort the tops into pullovers (camisoles, T-shirts, sweaters, etc.) and those that open at the front (blouses with buttons or zippers, cardigans, hoodies, etc.). Then sort them further into heavyweight and lightweight.

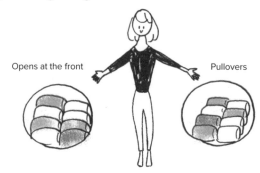

Opens at the front · Pullovers

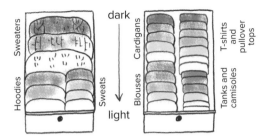

Store the sorted tops upright, with their colour in mind

You may need multiple drawers for tops since they tend to be larger in number and type. In that case, separating them into lightweight and heavyweight makes it easier to find things later. Group them by type inside each drawer and arrange them so that the lightest colours go at the front and the darker ones at the back.

Sort the bottoms by shape, then by the texture of the material

Sort bottoms by type (trousers, skirts, dresses, etc.) then by texture of the material (lightweight vs. heavyweight, or cotton-like vs. wool-like). It's helpful to make denim its own category.

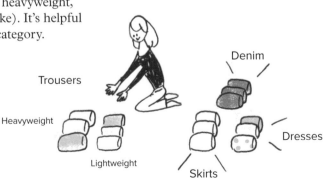

Store the sorted bottoms upright, with the colour in mind

First, divide the drawer into vertical rows by clothing type (trousers, skirts, dresses, etc.). Then store each piece upright from back to front, with the heavier weights in the back. At the same time, think about creating a dark-to-light gradient from back to front.

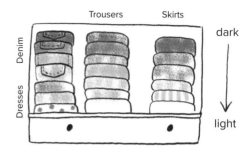

Store bras like royalty

Bras are exquisite garments that envelop women's precious breasts and uplift their mood. In that sense, they're more like an invisible accessory than a piece of clothing. Store them with care, without squishing or folding them. Because bras deserve a special treatment, I recommend arranging them a little differently from other clothes: place the darker, deeper colours at the front and place the lighter colours at the back.

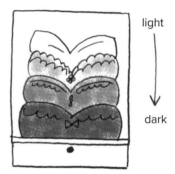

Keep bras in their own compartment
If you're going to store bras and other items in the same drawer, create a separate compartment just for bras with a box, etc. so that they don't get mixed up. Bras are considered royalty, and their storage needs to reflect a sense of specialness.

Use small boxes for pants and tights

Small boxes are useful for storing pants, tights and other items made from thin materials. A tissue box is a perfect container for pants, and a shoe box is great for tights. As with other types of clothing, arrange them from back to front, dark to light.

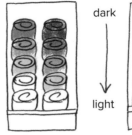

dark

↓

light

Organize the drawers according to content weight

When organizing drawers, start with the heavy items (bottoms, heavy knit pieces, etc.) in the bottom drawer. Then arrange the rest so that the content becomes lighter as you go up (lightweight tops, komono, etc.). As royalty, bras should of course be in one of the top drawers. This way, the entire set radiates an uplifting energy.

Don't keep socks or underwear in the bathroom!

Have you been storing socks or underwear in the bathroom for easy access after a shower? These don't belong in the bathroom or any other public space where other people enter. Instead, keep them in the privacy of your bedroom, along with all your other clothes.

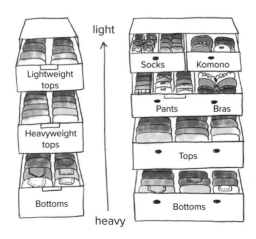

light

↑

Lightweight tops

Heavyweight tops

Bottoms

Socks Komono

Pants Bras

Tops

Bottoms

heavy

Store everything else in the wardrobe

Place hats on the top shelf to keep their shape

Shaped hats should be stacked and placed on the top shelf so that they don't get squashed. Knitted hats can be folded in half or thirds and stored in a basket for clothing accessories.

Hanging clothes

Are you taking good care of the clothes on hangers, making sure that the hem doesn't get caught in anything? Adjust the position of the drawers and shelves so that everything is nice and organized.

Pack clothes for specific events in a sealed container and tuck it away

When it comes to clothes for special events, it's okay to store them at the back of the wardrobe where it's harder to access, because you'll know where they are when you need them. I recommend putting them together in a container with a lid.

Folded clothes

Pack them comfortably in the drawer so they can enjoy a nice rest. Place the dresser or drawer unit where it doesn't obstruct the hanging clothes.

Organize the wardrobe in such a way that makes you excited to open it. Once you've finished hanging the clothes on hangers and putting away the folded clothes in the drawers, it's time to store the rest of the items, including clothing accessories and clothes for specific events. At this point, if you find yourself unable to handle any of the items with proper care, pause and do another joy check on it.

Line up the bags on the top shelf

Using the bag-in-bag method, line up the self-standing bags on the top shelf. The box of folded cloth bags can be tucked in wherever space is available, such as above a drawer unit.

Put gloves and other accessories in a basket to save space

Keep gloves, foldable hats, and other accessories together in a basket. Storing them folded and in an upright position makes them easy to reach for in those last moments before leaving the house.

Make a place for the things you carry around every day

Are you giving your everyday bag a chance to rest? Create a holding space for pouches, card cases, and anything else you usually carry, so that you can empty your bag and let it rest every time you come home.

Keep empty boxes and drawers until the very end

Storage boxes that were emptied in the tidying process may be used to store things in other categories down the line, whether temporarily or permanently. They can come in surprisingly handy, so hold on to them until your entire tidying marathon is finished.

STEP 4

Store the shoes

Utilize storage items on tall shelves

Although my general recommendation is to keep storage simple without using commercial storage items, there are a few exceptions. For a tall shelf, you can use a self-standing shelf to divide it into two levels. If you have a lot of depth in the shelf, try storing each pair with one shoe in front of the other, using a tension rod to lift up the front shoe.

Minimize the number of shoes in the hallway

A cluttered hallway blocks airflow and stifles the entire house. Limit the shoes in the hallway to one pair per person: the one they wore that day and needs to be aired out.

The final task for clothing storage is to put away the shoes in the shoe cabinet. To create a sense of balance, place the pairs that give off a heavier impression at the bottom, then work your way up so that you finish with the lightest pairs at the top. Ideally you'll have plenty of room to simply lay out the shoes on each shelf, but if not, get creative: bring in some store-bought organizers or move some of the less frequently used pairs to the wardrobe, for example.

Men's shoes at the bottom, children's and women's at the top

To balance out a family shoe rack, group the shoes for each person and place the bigger and heavier men's shoes below, and smaller and lighter children's and women's shoes above. Women's boots can go on the bottom shelf as well.

Use a box for thin, sturdy shoes

You can fit two pairs of flip flops or other thin yet sturdy shoes in one box to save space. The box can then sit nicely on the shelf.

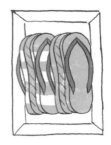

Clean and move some shoes to the wardrobe as needed

If you can't fit all the shoes on the shoe rack because you live with a large family, put the less frequently used pairs in boxes and move them to the wardrobe. Make sure to clean the soles and let them dry out beforehand.

Reflection: tidying clothes

Congratulations! You've now finished tidying your clothes. How are you feeling? Perhaps you are still in shock after seeing the mountain of clothes you had accumulated. You may also be feeling fatigue. But look around and take in what you've accomplished: the wardrobe and drawers neatly packed only with clothes that you love. You may feel an ineffable sense of fulfillment and peace.

Write down how you're feeling, and add photos or illustrations of the transformed storage spaces. Having a record of your progress in this way is sure to give you the motivation you need to continue on your tidying journey.

Completed worksheet example

How was tidying clothes for you?

Write down how you feel now that you've actually tidied, what you want to do going forward, the next steps, and your intention for tidying the next category.

1. Describe how you feel now in a few words.

> I did it!

Why? I've been ignoring the clutter until now, but focusing on joy helped me feel good about letting things go!

2. What changes would you like to make in your wardrobe? Example: get a few more 'grown-up' items

• More colour variation for tops
• Get new underwear
• Add form-fitting clothes (because most of mine are relaxed fit . . .)

3. What changes would you like to make in your clothing storage? Example: replace all hangers with a uniform set

• Replace the accessories basket with a prettier one
• Organize the inside of the wardrobe so it's easier to clean

4. What is your intention for tidying the next category (books)?

> There are so many books I'm reluctant to throw away, but I'm willing to face them head on!

Make note of things to add or improve regarding your wardrobe or storage.

Write down how you honestly feel and reflect on the reason why.

82

How was tidying clothes for you?

Write down how you feel now that you've actually tidied, what you want to do going forward, the next steps, and your intention for tidying the next category.

1. Describe how you feel now in a few words.

Why?
_____
_____
_____
_____

2. What changes would you like to make in your wardrobe?

Example: get a few more 'grown-up' items

_____
_____
_____
_____
_____
_____
_____
_____
_____

3. What changes would you like to make in your clothing storage? Example: replace all hangers with a uniform set

_____
_____
_____
_____
_____
_____
_____

4. What is your intention for tidying the next category (books)?

Completed worksheet example

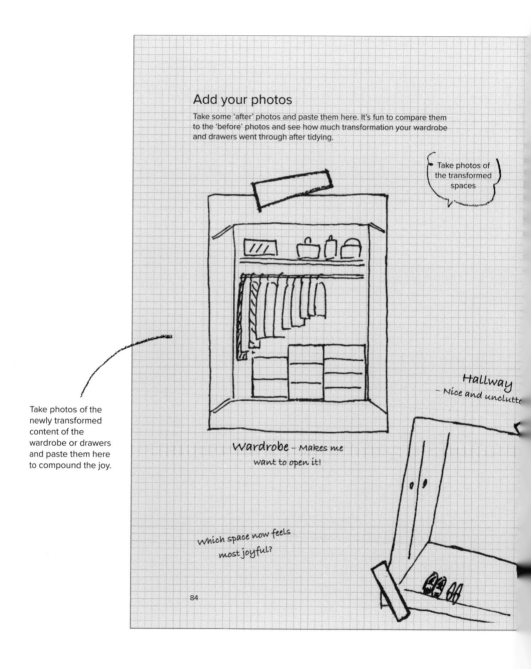

Add your photos

Take some 'after' photos and paste them here. It's fun to compare them to the 'before' photos and see how much transformation your wardrobe and drawers went through after tidying.

Take photos of the transformed spaces

Take photos of the newly transformed content of the wardrobe or drawers and paste them here to compound the joy.

Wardrobe – Makes me want to open it!

Hallway – Nice and unclutte

Which space now feels most joyful?

84

What are your top 3 clothes that spark the most joy? Add a photo or an illustration

Use words and illustrations to record any observations, thoughts or a list of clothes that you particularly love.

I'll wear them with loving care

The tops drawer – much better appearance and accessibility!

Put the joy you feel into words

Add your photos

Take some 'after' photos and paste them here. It's fun to compare them to the 'before' photos and see how much transformation your wardrobe and drawers went through after tidying.

Take photos of the transformed spaces

What are your
top 3 clothes that
spark the most joy?
Add a photo or an
illustration

Put the joy you
feel into words

Chapter 3

Tidy your books

We tend to accumulate books without realizing; they're one of the three things people have the hardest time discarding.

A surprising number of people say books are the one thing they just can't part with. But this also means that, once you've handpicked only the books that spark joy and cleared out everything else, you'll enjoy a sense of exhilaration unlike any other. And soon you'll notice a clear difference in the quality of information that you receive.

Fill in the dates when you started and finished

Started _____ (year) _____ (month) _____ (day) at _____ (time)

Finished _____ (year) _____ (month) _____ (day) at _____ (time)

How to tidy without relapsing

The key is to take all your books off the shelves and lay them on the floor. Don't be lazy enough to skip this part, or you'll have a harder time with the joy check. Once you've made your selection, place them back on the bookshelf with loving care.

1. Gather

Take out all your books and gather them in one place to wake them up

Books that have been sitting on the shelf without being read are essentially asleep. This makes it hard to discern whether or not to keep them, so remove them from the shelf and wake them up. If you have too many books to fit on the floor, you can tackle one genre at a time.

If there are too many, do one genre at a time

The 'joy check' order

It's fine to start with whichever books feel the easiest, but if you have too many and can't tidy them all at once, do your joy check by subcategory, as you did with clothing. General books (what you read for fun) are a good place to start; since it tends to be the biggest subcategory, you can feel productive right off the bat.

General
Books you read for fun, including novels, essays and comics. Do you have any old books sleeping that you'd completely forgotten about or are looking all sad and discoloured?

2. Keep what sparks joy

Touch each book and let your heart decide!

Once you've laid the books on the floor, hold them in your hands one by one and ask yourself if it sparks joy. Do not open the book while doing this, as reading the content will cloud your judgement. Look only at the cover and title, and make your decision quickly based on whether you feel uplifted when you touch it. Throughout the process, hold a vision of your bookcase filled only with the books that you love.

Practical
Travel guides, reference books, etc. If you have ones that you keep meaning to read 'when you have the time' but never get around to it, ask yourself: 'Is that true?' and 'When?'

Visual
Photo books, catalogues, newsletters and other visual-oriented publications. If only a portion sparks joy, cut it out and keep it in a folder.

Magazines
Whether it's fashion or information, magazines generally have a very brief 'season'. Cut out and keep only the pages that spark joy. If you subscribe to a magazine, get in the habit of doing a joy check on each issue as soon as you finish reading it.

3. Store

Store what you've chosen in a joyful state

Books that spark joy need to be stored in a way that feels uplifting. Keep them upright instead of stacking them flat. See if you can arrange them in such a way that looks nice and cohesive, by paying attention to the height and colour of the spine and removing any glaring dust jackets or belly bands.

Don't read books while you tidy them!

Gather all books in one pile and write down your observations

Example:
- There was a huge pile of magazines in the corner of my room
- I found ten books that I hadn't even finished!

_____

_____

_____

_____

_____

_____

_____

_____

_____

_____

Reading it 'one day' means 'never'

If you've been leaving a book unread or unfinished for a long time, you've likely already missed the window of time to read it. People say 'I'll read this one day', but that 'one day' will never come. If you really want to read it, I recommend setting an actual timeframe to do so.

Are there any books that you've never read?

Touch each one and keep only what sparks joy

Once all the books are laid out on the floor, I sometimes go around slapping the covers to wake them up before doing the joy check. It's a fun little ritual that somehow makes it easier to judge which books spark joy. Give it a try!

Slap, slap

Z zz...

Give thanks to what doesn't spark joy and let it go

Give a rough estimate, e.g. '30 books' or 'one moving box full'

Leave photo albums and other people's books alone for now

Your bookcase may also contain photo albums, yearbooks, diaries or books that belong to other members of the household. Don't try to tidy these just yet! Photo albums and things that have sentimental value belong in their own category (see p.85). As for books that aren't yours, let the respective owner make their own decisions. Focus on your own books first.

'Joy check' tips for books

Discerning books that spark joy just by touching them may feel tricky at first. Here are some tips to help you get the hang of it.

If you really can't tell, flip through the book for ten seconds only

Sometimes you just can't tell if the book sparks joy, even after taking all the right steps. If that's the case, try glancing at the table of contents or flipping through the pages for just ten seconds. Set your own parameters to help yourself make decisions more easily. That said, don't get carried away reading it!

Series: stack them up and do a single joy check

For serialized novels and comics, don't worry about going through each volume separately. Stack up the entire series, then do your joy check by putting your arms around the pile or just taking the one volume at the top. Be careful about flipping through them though, or you'll likely get distracted!

Cut out only the pages that spark joy and put them in a folder

If only a portion of a magazine sparks joy, cut that part out and keep it temporarily in a folder. You may look at it later and wonder why on earth you kept it, as often happens with clippings. Remember to do another joy check on them when you tidy papers (see p.90).

Proudly keep the books in your personal hall of fame

If you can't bear to say goodbye to a book that's falling apart because you've loved it so much since childhood – that's your bible! It doesn't matter what anyone else says; if it's a book you want to cherish, keep it proudly. And to honour the joy these books bring you, list them below.

What books belong in your personal hall of fame?

_____

_____

_____

_____

_____

_____

_____

_____

_____

_____

_____

Store your chosen books attractively

Once you've narrowed down your book collection to only what sparks joy, it's time to store them in a way that makes them shine. It's fine to do this whatever way you like, but I recommend keeping the books upright rather than stacking them horizontally. See if you can add subtle arrangements by height or colour so that they look nice and cohesive – it'll make you happy every time you walk past them!

Group the books by category

Instead of randomly laying out your book collection, group them by category: novels, references, magazines and so on. This gives each category a uniform look and makes it easier to see what's where.

Arrange books by height or colour

Once you've grouped the books according to category, it's nice to arrange them by increasing height from left to right, or by colour to create a gradient. These small touches can add so much spark to book storage.

Don't worry if you still have a lot of books

If you still feel like you have too many books after you've finished tidying, no problem. Honing your sensitivity to joy takes time. You can always refine your selection if you realize later that some of them don't actually spark joy.

Remove the dust jacket if the book collection doesn't look cohesive

You've laid out your book collection nicely on the bookshelf, but something still doesn't look right. If that's the case, try removing the jacket or belly band, as they tend to have bold colours that can be quite distracting. This alone should make a big difference to the overall aesthetic. Of course, feel free to leave them on if they spark joy for you.

When books are stacked on their sides, the ones at the bottom are likely to be left unread, so the rule of thumb is to store them upright and in one location. That said, it's fine to store certain books in a different location if that's the only place where they'll be used – you may want to keep your cookbooks in the kitchen, for example.

Reflection: tidying books

I had a hard time discarding books myself, so I know how challenging it can be. But if you bite the bullet and keep only what sparks joy, you'll notice your mind becoming wonderfully clear and refreshed. Tidying books helps you catch the exact information you need when you need it. You become more sensitive to information when you don't accumulate too many books.

Take some time to reflect on your thoughts and feelings now, so that you can attract the perfect book at exactly the right time in the future. It's also a good idea to list the books you want to read right now.

Completed worksheet example

Describe in a few words how you feel after tidying, e.g. 'So clean!' or 'Feels great!' and consider the reason why.

Think about how you want to manage books now that you've finished tidying them. Then set an intention for tidying the next category: papers.

How was tidying books for you?

Write down how you honestly feel now that you've finished
tidying books, any changes you want to make going forward,
and your intention for taking the next step.

1. Describe how you feel now
in a few words.

Why? _____

_____

_____

_____

_____

2. What changes would you like
to make regarding books and
magazines? Example: take time to
enjoy history books

_____

_____

_____

_____

_____

_____

_____

_____

_____

3. What changes would you like
to make in your book storage?
Example: make better use of the
available space

_____

_____

_____

_____

_____

_____

_____

_____

4. What is your intention for tidying
the next category: paper?

Add your photos

Once you've laid out only the books you love, take some 'after' photos to see how much transformation your book collection went through. Notice the dramatic difference in the before and after, even though they both contain books of the same rectangular shape.

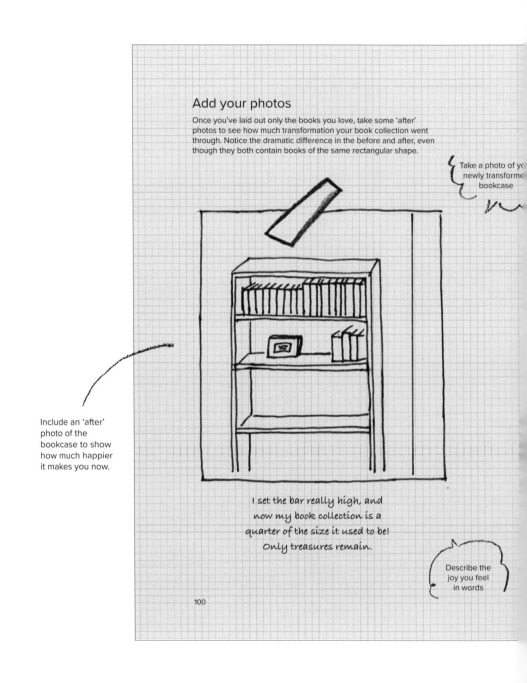

Take a photo of y
newly transforme
bookcase

Include an 'after' photo of the bookcase to show how much happier it makes you now.

I set the bar really high, and now my book collection is a quarter of the size it used to be! Only treasures remain.

Describe the joy you feel in words

The children's book I
bought when I was in
school

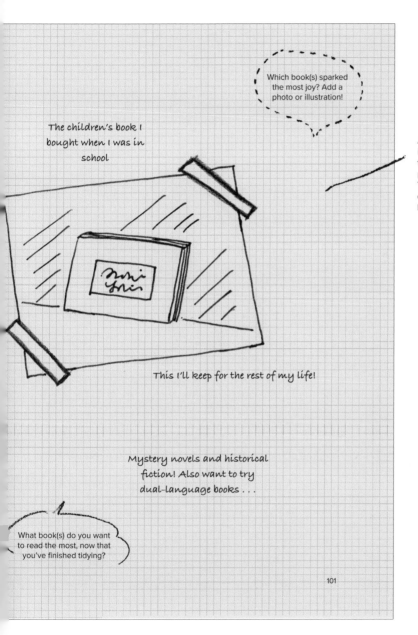

Which book(s) sparked
the most joy? Add a
photo or illustration!

Add a photo or
illustration to honour
the books in your
personal hall of fame.
You can also write
down the title of the
books in big letters.

This I'll keep for the rest of my life!

Mystery novels and historical
fiction! Also want to try
dual-language books . . .

What book(s) do you want
to read the most, now that
you've finished tidying?

101

Add your photos

Once you've laid out only the books you love, take some 'after' photos to see how much transformation your book collection went through. Notice the dramatic difference in the before and after, even though they both contain books of the same rectangular shape.

Take a photo of your newly transformed bookcase

Describe the joy you feel in words

Which book(s) sparked the most joy? Add a photo or illustration!

What book(s) do you want to read the most, now that you've finished tidying?

Chapter 4

Tidy your papers

Now that you've tidied your clothes and books, let's move on to your papers. My basic rule for sorting papers: discard everything! Papers accumulate easily, so we need to be that stringent when making our selection. Documents like contracts obviously have nothing to do with joy, so keep only what you need.

Fill in the dates when you started and finished

Started _____ (year) _____ (month) _____ (day) at _____ (time)

Finished _____ (year) _____ (month) _____ (day) at _____ (time)

How to tidy without relapsing

'Papers' include everything from contracts to post, takeaway menus, flyers, and any other printed materials except stationery. Go through them one by one dispassionately and decide if it's something you really need to keep.

1. Gather

Gather all papers pertaining to you from every corner of the house

There are certain spots in a house where papers tend to pile up like snowdrifts, such as the top of the table or the corner of the kitchen counter. Check these areas and everywhere else for any piece of paper that you are responsible for, and gather them all in one place.

Write down your observations after removing all your papers

Example:
• Lots of old takeaway menus
• I stick everything on the fridge that I don't know what to do with

_____

_____

_____

_____

_____

_____

_____

_____

_____

_____

_____

There's more over here!

2. Keep what you need

Consider the timeframe of use and keep only what you need

Any paper worth keeping belongs to one of three categories: 'currently using', 'needed for a limited period', and 'keep indefinitely'. Everything else you don't need. Stay away from letters or photographs for now, as these are considered sentimental items (p.174) that we will tackle last.

Shred sensitive documents before discarding

Protect your personal information by shredding all documents that contain your name, address, date of birth, bank accounts, identification numbers, etc. before discarding them. Use a shredder or tear them by hand into small pieces.

Tips for tough paper decisions

There are so many different types of paper documents, and for some it's harder to discern if it's okay to throw them away. Here are some pointers for dealing with the tricky categories my private clients often ask about.

Used cheque books

Unless you need them for tax returns, simply ask yourself if flipping through them sparks joy. If you think you might need them in the future, decide how many years to keep them for.

Course materials

Have you ever reread them after finishing the course? The value of any course lies in the excitement you feel while taking it and in applying what you learned to your work or personal life. Let go of anything that has already served its purpose.

Credit card statements

You have no need for credit card statements once you've looked through them and extracted the information for bookkeeping purposes. Throw them away unless you need them for tax returns. Switching to electronic statements is a great idea.

Clippings

This is the time to go through the clippings you filed away while tidying books (p.95) as well. Keep what you've chosen in a presentation book with clear plastic sleeves or have fun making a scrapbook.

Manuals and warranties

These days you can view most household electronic manuals online. All you really need is to keep the unexpired warranties in a clear plastic folder or a box.

Pay stubs

Pay stubs have fulfilled their duty the moment you confirmed the content. This, too, can be disposed of immediately unless you need them for tax returns. If you're going to hold on to them, set a time limit and stick to it.

Greeting cards

Once you've opened and read a greeting card, its job is done. As for Japanese New Year's cards with lottery numbers, check to see if the numbers won anything, then say thank you and goodbye. If you use the cards as an address book for the following year, then save only one year's worth. If the card sparks joy, group them with sentimental items (p.174).

Give thanks to the papers you don't need and let them go

Give a rough estimate, e.g. 'one bin bag full'

No need for
an elaborate
filing system!

3. Store

Store papers in three categories

Once you've made your selection, sort the remaining papers into three categories: important but rarely used legal documents such as contracts, more frequently used papers you need to save, and lastly, papers that require action. Keep each category together in a box or a folder so that they don't get scattered about.

Contracts and legal documents = Save

Other important documents = Save

Pending = Aim to keep it empty

Assign a day to attend to pending documents

The pending box needs to be empty by default. Set aside a day to process its contents in one sitting, whether it's writing a reply to a letter or updating information with service providers. You'll feel much better if you take care of this before you move on to the next category of komono.

Important legal documents such as contracts

Legal documents such as insurance policies, rental agreements and household electronics warranties need to be saved, but you won't be looking at them frequently. Simply keep them together in a box or clear plastic folder.

Non-legal papers you want to save

This category encompasses all papers besides legal documents that you need to keep, including school or work calendar and hobby-related papers such as recipe clippings. It's best to sort these by category and store them in presentation books with clear plastic sleeves for easy browsing.

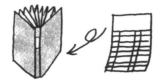

Pending

Create a pending box to keep all papers that require action in one place. This includes payment slips and anything that you need to respond to. I recommend using a standing magazine holder that keeps papers upright and easy to access.

List of documents with expiration dates

List the papers you are saving for a limited time period, such as household electronics warranties and documents you need for tax return purposes, so that you don't forget to throw them away when the time comes.

_____

Keep until _____ (year) _____ (month) _____ (day)

_____

Keep until _____ (year) _____ (month) _____ (day)

_____

Keep until _____ (year) _____ (month) _____ (day)

_____

Keep until _____ (year) _____ (month) _____ (day)

_____

Keep until _____ (year) _____ (month) _____ (day)

_____

Keep until _____ (year) _____ (month) _____ (day)

_____

Keep until _____ (year) _____ (month) _____ (day)

_____

Keep until _____ (year) _____ (month) _____ (day)

_____

Keep until _____ (year) _____ (month) _____ (day)

_____

Keep until _____ (year) _____ (month) _____ (day)

Are you sure you need to keep all of these?

How was tidying papers for you?

Write down how you feel now that you've straightened out your paper clutter. Take time to reflect on how you'd like to manage papers going forward and your intentions for tidying komono (miscellaneous items) next.

1. Describe how you feel now in a few words.

Why?

2. What changes would you like to make regarding papers?

Example: tidy pending documents regularly!

3. What changes would you like to make in your paper storage? Example: organize papers for the whole family once I'm done with my tidying

4. What is your intention for tidying the next category: komono (miscellaneous items)?

Chapter 5

Tidy your komono

From stationery to cosmetics, kitchen tools, medication, cleaning products and everything in between, just thinking about the sheer number and variety of komono (miscellaneous items) can make our heads spin. But not to worry. Having made it this far, you've been steadily honing your tidying skills and sensitivity to joy. Just believe in yourself and follow the workbook page by page – and all your komono will be tidied up in no time.

Fill in the dates when you started and finished

Started _____ (year) _____ (month) _____ (day) at _____ (time)

Finished _____ (year) _____ (month) _____ (day) at _____ (time)

How to tidy without relapsing

Komono is vast in numbers, so do your joy check by subcategory. Pick out the items you actively want to have in your everyday life, from a pile of things you have 'just because'.

1. Gather

Gather the items that belong to you personally by category

The key to conquering the vast assortment of komono is to know your categories. Simply follow the basic steps: gather them in the order specified below, choose what sparks joy, and store them. Include all items that you're in charge of, even if they are being used by the whole family.

First

Next

The 'joy check' order

The number of komono in a house can seem insurmountable, so the trick is to start with the more personal and easily classified items. If you live alone, that means everything is your personal belonging, so don't worry about the order; start with the category that feels easiest for you to sort through.

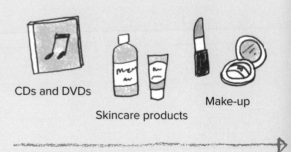

CDs and DVDs

Skincare products

Make-up

2. Keep what sparks joy

Making tough decisions increases your sensitivity to joy

As you go through your komono, you'll likely come across items in the grey area: things that don't spark joy per se but are still necessary. When that happens, refer to the following guidelines and take some time to really think about what to keep. This process will further hone your sensitivity to joy.

Is it useful?

Keep empty boxes for storage

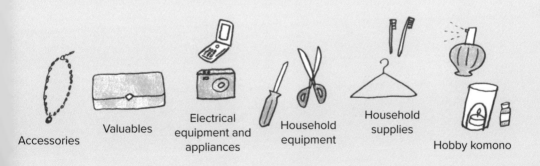

Accessories

Valuables

Electrical equipment and appliances

Household equipment

Household supplies

Hobby komono

Stationery goes in this drawer!

3. Store

Store komono by category in a way that makes it easy to put them back

To keep your room nice and tidy, gather all komono in the same category in one spot and decide where to store every item. Instead of buying commercial organizers, start by using empty boxes to divide drawers and shelves. Position things upright whenever possible, and store them in a way that makes it easy to put them back.

Komono to keep

Useful items that spark joy

If a useful item sparks joy without a doubt, keep it with confidence and put it to good use in your daily life. The more often you use something that makes your heart swoon, the happier you feel.

Not-so-useful items that spark joy

If something sparks joy, keep it proudly. Even if you don't use it, have fun decorating with it: put it on display, hang it, or pin it to the wall.

Necessary items that don't spark joy

Try to think of as many reasons as you can why that item makes your life easier and what purpose it serves. If you find its unassuming appearance comforting or appreciate how handy it is when you need it, it can be considered to be bringing you joy. Go ahead and keep it.

Kitchen goods and food supplies

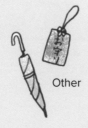

Other

Designate a home for every komono

Decide where to store your komono

When figuring out storage, the underlying assumption should be that you will designate a spot for every single item in the house and put it back there after using it. I recommend referring back to the storage floorplan you sketched out on p.31 as you decide where to keep your komono.

If you fail to assign a home for even one item and leave it out in some random spot, it's game over – that one item will attract more and more stuff to it like a magnet, and your room will revert to clutter in no time. For this reason, designating storage location determines whether or not you can live your ideal lifestyle.

That said, storage placements should be finalized only after you've finished sorting through all of your komono. Until then, you can relax and let all storage be temporary.

How to determine where to store your komono

Don't scatter storage spaces

The KonMari Method's rule for storage is simple: store all items in the same category in one place, and don't let them scatter about. If you live with family, give each person a dedicated storage space or spaces, then store their belongings by category within each. As an exception to this rule, items that are used only in certain locations can be stored separately from the rest of their category.

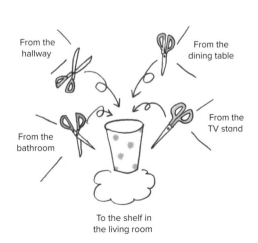

From the hallway

From the dining table

From the bathroom

From the TV stand

To the shelf in the living room

Don't overcategorize them by frequency of use

Trying too hard to sort items by various frequency of use can result in confusion and stalling in the midst of tidying. All you really need is two groups: frequently used items, and everything else. From there, you can always make adjustments as you go through your day-to-day life, such as moving the items you use frequently towards the front.

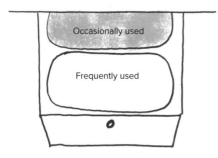

Store things in a way that looks comfortable

When objects in storage look uncomfortable – packed like sardines or exposed to a lot of moisture, for example – this is bound to make you relapse back into clutter. When deciding on storage locations, think not only about convenience but also giving your possessions a comfortable home.

Store things upright instead of stacking

Storing things in an upright position so as to avoid overlapping makes it easier to manage them and grasp how much you have. Once you start stacking things on top of each other, they'll keep piling up endlessly. The poor objects at the bottom get crushed, worn out and eventually forgotten. So do your best to avoid stacking!

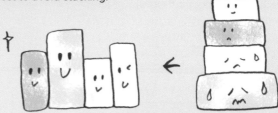

Determine where to store each komono by association

Deciding where to store each komono is like playing a word association game. Let's say you've decided where to keep the electrical cords. You might then place your computer nearby, because they're in the same 'electrical' family. And since you use your computer every day, you might want to keep your favourite stationery next to it, and so on. It's like stringing together items of similar categories.

Make the most out of built-in storage

When designing storage, refer to your floorplan on p.31 and start by filling built-in storage such as cupboards. Instead of leaving shelving units or clothing racks out in the open, see if you can slip them into the built-in storage, so that your room feels extra spacious.

While still tidying, storage can be temporary

Until you finish sorting through everything, you won't know the total amount nor how best to categorize them. So don't expect to figure out all storage locations at once. If you want to put things away to make room for day-to-day activities while still tidying, let that storage be temporary.

CDs and DVDs

I put CDs and DVDs first in line when tidying komono, because they belong to the same family of communication media as books and papers, which makes them just as easy to sort through. A CD or DVD you received as a gift can be hard to throw away, even if you don't love it. Take a moment to appreciate the memories it brings up, then let it go with gratitude. Whatever you do, don't start watching it or listening to it!

Gather all items in one pile and write down your observations

Example:
- So many albums of a pop star I no longer care for
- Found a DVD I rented and forgot to return...

Touch each one and keep only what sparks joy

As with books, do your joy check by holding each one in your hands. Any CD with an album cover you get so much joy out of is of course worth keeping, even if you don't listen to it anymore.

Sort by colour

Give thanks to what doesn't spark joy and let it go

Give a rough estimate, e.g. '50 CDs' or '20 DVDs'

Store what you've chosen in an attractive manner without stacking

Don't stack the discs horizontally; store them upright on the shelf or in the drawer, perhaps arranging them by colour. If you only have a handful, you can put them in a basket instead. Putting your absolute favourites on display with the album cover showing can be a nice touch.

Put your favourites on display

If you want to digitize the content, put it in the 'pending box'

If want to transfer the data to your computer from a CD or DVD before tossing it, put it in the pending box that you created for papers (p.111), and make a point to take care of it as soon as possible.

Skincare products

Skincare products are water-based, so it's best to use them while they're still fresh. Once they start to grow old, be decisive and throw them away, or, if it's a face-care product, you can apply what's left of them lavishly on your body. Although the standard storage location for skincare products is the bathroom, where they're normally used, if you don't have enough space there, you can make a special spot for them in the cupboard or on the shelf.

Gather all items in one pile and write down your observations

Example:
- Found a pile of skincare samples
- Shocked to see an expensive beauty serum had changed colour

Touch each one and keep only what sparks joy

Gather all skincare products and check to see if they spark joy. If something doesn't speak to your heart now, it's time to toss it, even if it's still usable.

For skincare products, freshness is everything

The fresher the skincare product, the more joy it sparks when you use it. Skincare samples tend to accumulate and degrade while you keep them stocked up, so now's the time to make the call on whether to use them right away or chuck them.

Give thanks to what doesn't spark joy and let it go

Give a rough estimate, e.g. '20 samples' or '3 bottles'

Keep what you've chosen separate from make-up

Skincare products are usually watery, whereas make-up products are more powdery – so store them separately. Use a small box to keep the tubes and other little bits and pieces together, letting them stand upright. If you have a big collection, you may choose to separate the ones you use daily from those reserved for special treatments.

Keep the bits and pieces in a small box

Make-up

For many, applying make-up is a daily ritual for bringing out your feminine essence, so select the tools for it based on how much joy they bring you, first and foremost. For storage, arrange them in a way that looks pretty, so that you'll feel a surge of joy every time you use them. Dirty containers are a downer, so be sure to always keep them nice and clean.

Any make-up samples you haven't used in a year?

Have you been stocking up on make-up samples, thinking they'd come in handy for travelling? Yet they are hardly ever used in reality. Samples only contain a small amount and spoil easily, so it's best to toss them unless you're going to use them immediately.

Gather all items in one pile and write down your observations

Example:
• Lots of half-used eyeshadows
• Found a bottle of nail polish that was hardened and unusable

Touch each one and keep only what sparks joy

Make-up often plays a big role in bringing more joy to a woman's life. Set your bar quite high when selecting what to keep. Discard anything that's old or doesn't suit your current taste.

Store what you've chosen in an attractive manner

Store make-up brushes, mascaras and other items upright whenever possible. Using a beautiful box or glassware is a wonderful idea. As for the rest of the items, divide them by type and store them in an aesthetically pleasing way.

Give thanks to what doesn't spark joy and let it go

Give a rough estimate, e.g. '3 foundations' or '2 lipsticks'

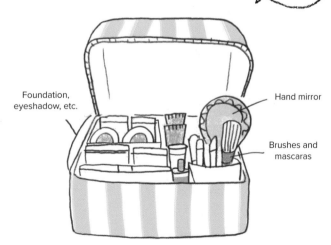

Separate items that can be stored upright from everything else

Foundation, eyeshadow, etc.

Hand mirror

Brushes and mascaras

Accessories

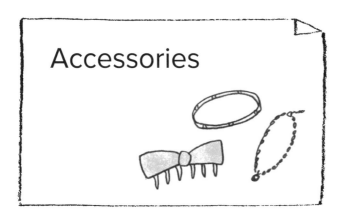

Accessories exist to make you sparkle – they are essentially the queen among all komono. Handle them with extra care during your joy check, and offer them heartfelt respect and gratitude when you let them go. For storage, lay them out attractively like a shop display, so that they look just as beautiful while on standby. Wrist watches are included in this category as well.

Set aside meaningful pieces as 'sentimental items'

Whether it's the ring from your ex or the accessory your friend made by hand, items that hold special meaning can bring your tidying process to a halt if you don't handle them at the right time. Set them aside as 'sentimental items' to go through later (p.171).

Gather all items in one pile and write down your observations

Example:
• Found a rusty necklace
• Lots of earrings missing the other half

_____

_____

_____

_____

_____

_____

_____

_____

_____

_____

_____

_____

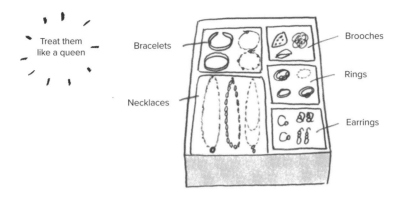

Treat them like a queen

Bracelets

Necklaces

Brooches

Rings

Earrings

Touch each one and keep only what sparks joy

During the joy check, you may come across something that you've outworn but still love the charm that came with it. In that case, it's always an option to keep just the part that sparks joy.

Store what you've chosen in an attractive manner

There are three ways to store accessories: drawers (e.g. dressers), boxes (e.g. jewellery box or cosmetic bag) or display (e.g. hang on the wall). Whichever you choose, store them appealingly by type.

Give thanks to what doesn't spark joy and let it go

e.g. '5 brooches' or '8 pairs of earrings'

Group hair accessories by type

While you're on accessories, don't forget to include those that adorn your hair. Once you've chosen which ones spark joy, sort them by type and store each group in its own compartment (hair ties, bobby pins, clips, barrettes, etc.) so that they look nice and organized.

Hair ties

Barrettes and clips

Bobby pins

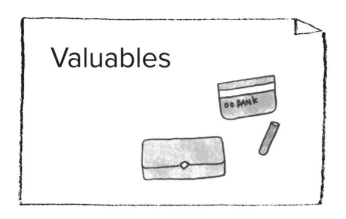

Valuables

Types of valuables include financial items (cash, the cheque book currently in use, cards, gift cards, foreign currency etc.), cards (credit cards, health insurance cards, loyalty cards etc.) and IDs (passports, pension handbook etc.). Being valuable, they need to be stored properly with respect.

Check the expiry dates

Check the date on loyalty cards etc. and throw them away if they're expired. If you come across something that can be exchanged for cash, put it in the pending box you made on p.111 so that you don't forget.

Gather all items in one pile and write down your observations

Example:
- So many loyalty cards I never use
- Found a gift card I had completely forgotten about

_____

_____

_____

_____

_____

_____

_____

_____

_____

_____

_____

_____

Wallets and bras are royalty

Even among valuables, wallets are in a class of their own, as they're the home of money. I consider them royalty, much like bras. My daily wallet ritual involves removing the receipts, wrapping it in a piece of fabric, and storing it in its designated box as I say to it aloud, 'Thank you for your hard work!'

Give thanks to what doesn't spark joy and let it go

Give a rough estimate, e.g. '10 expired coupons'

Touch each one and keep only what sparks joy

The selection criterion for valuables should be more about practicality than joy. Even so, hold each one in your hand and look at them closely to determine if it's something you need.

Store what you've chosen in a proper manner

Valuable items should be stored in a respectable place. They pair well with safes, drawers, and wooden boxes. You can also use a pouch if you don't have that many. For cards, I recommend using a small box to keep them upright. If you're concerned about security, store your cheque book and any online banking widgets separately.

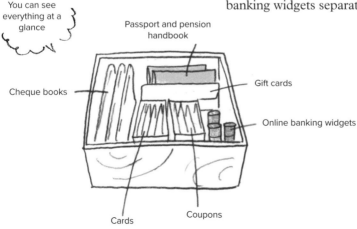

You can see everything at a glance

Passport and pension handbook

Cheque books

Gift cards

Online banking widgets

Cards

Coupons

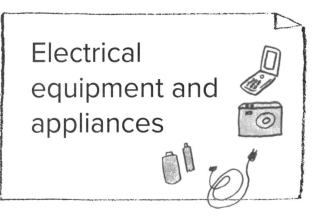

Electrical equipment and appliances

This category includes computers, digital cameras, electronic dictionaries, mobile phones, memory cards, skincare devices, batteries and anything that feels 'electrical'. That said, if you have a large number of things related to a hobby such as photography, it's fine to set them aside as hobby komono and go through them later (p.142).

Discard mysterious cables and packing boxes immediately

Whether it's a charger for the camera or mobile phone that you no longer have, or the assortment of mysterious cables you threw in a bag, immediately discard anything with an unknown purpose. Packaging boxes should also be thrown away unless you can reuse them as storage compartments.

Gather all items in one pile and write down your observations

Example:
• Found a broken computer
• Lots of batteries

_____

_____

_____

_____

_____

_____

_____

_____

_____

_____

_____

_____

_____

_____

Touch each one and keep only what's necessary

Take this opportunity to get rid of broken mobile phones and computers that you've been keeping just because. If you find a memory card and need to upload the data to your computer, drop it into the pending box (p.111).

Give thanks to what doesn't spark joy and let it go

Give a rough estimate, e.g. '2 mobile phones', 'a handheld game console', or 'a facial device'

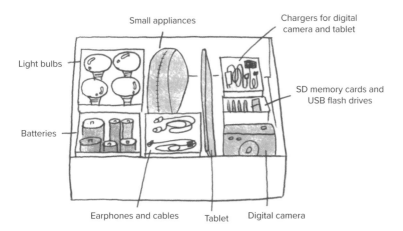

Small appliances

Chargers for digital camera and tablet

Light bulbs

SD memory cards and USB flash drives

Batteries

Earphones and cables   Tablet   Digital camera

Store what you've chosen, grouped together

You can store all 'electrical' items together in a drawer or box, even though they may vary greatly in size and shape. Keep them upright whenever possible. Put cables and small charger parts in a pouch so that they look nice and uncluttered. You may opt to store calculators and electronic dictionaries with stationery, which is classified as household equipment (p.134).

Household equipment

Stationery

Here we organize household equipment such as stationery, tools and sewing kits. There are many different kinds of stationery, so once you're done with the joy check, store them by subcategory (equipment, paper-related supplies and letter-writing supplies) to make it easier for you to put them back after using them. As for tools and sewing kits, you only need to keep a handful if you don't use them very often.

Gather all items in one pile and write down your observations

Example:
- Lots of half-used notebooks
- Found a whopping 10 red ballpoint pens!

Give thanks to what doesn't spark joy and let it go

Give a rough estimate, e.g. '20 pens', '5 memo pads', etc.

Touch each one and keep only what sparks joy

Pens tend to accumulate; test each one to make sure you can still write with it. If you have a bottle of liquid glue, check to see if it hasn't hardened.

Sort what you've chosen into three subcategories

Sort the remaining stationery into three subcategories: equipment (pens, scissors, staplers, etc.), paper-related supplies (notebooks, memo pads, post-it notes and folders for keeping papers together) and letter-writing supplies.

Equipment

Paper-related supplies

Letter-writing supplies

Store them with the three subcategories in mind

Stationery comes in a wide variety of types, materials and sizes. Hence it has a stronger affinity for partitioned storage than any other type of komono. Divide the space inside a drawer or box into as many compartments as needed, and place your stationery one by one, standing them up whenever possible. Using magazine folders is a good idea as well.

Notebooks and tall stationery:

Tall stationery in the paper or letter family, such as notebooks and letter papers, can be slipped into a magazine holder and placed upright next to the paper documents.

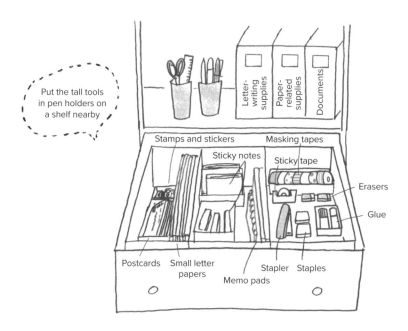

Put the tall tools in pen holders on a shelf nearby

Letter-writing supplies

Paper-related supplies

Documents

Stamps and stickers

Masking tapes

Sticky notes

Sticky tape

Erasers

Glue

Postcards

Small letter papers

Memo pads

Stapler

Staples

Letter-writing supplies:

Sort them by type (postcards, letter papers, notecard sets, etc.) and store them by height. Keep stickers and rubber stamps together as well.

Paper-related supplies:

Store notebooks or memo pads upright instead of stacking them horizontally. Place post-it notes and other small items upright in a box. Aim for storage that allows you to see where everything is at a glance.

Equipment:

Place masking tapes and glue sticks in a compact box so that they don't roll around. Keep the extra staples with the stapler. Pens can be laid on their sides if they're few in number.

Gather all items in one pile and write down your observations

Example:
• The sewing kit from primary school has been just sitting there
• Hadn't used the hammer in a while – it was covered in rust

_____

_____

_____

_____

_____

_____

_____

_____

_____

_____

Touch each one and keep only what sparks joy

Do you have bulky tools of unknown purpose just taking up space? Have you ever used that thimble or fabric marker in your sewing kit? If you don't foresee yourself using them, bid them all farewell.

Give thanks to what doesn't spark joy and let it go

Give a rough estimate, e.g. 'two grocery bags full'

Take care of all the pending repairs now
This is the perfect time to tighten that loose screw or sew on that missing button. It feels great to finally cross off all the repair and mending tasks that have been sitting on the to-do list.

Store what you've chosen in an attractive manner

Tools are tough by nature, so you can throw them all in a toolbox or a box and tuck them in wherever there's space. If you reduce them to the absolute minimum, they may even fit in a pouch. Sewing kits can be similarly organized in a sewing box or a pouch.

Household supplies

Next we sort through the essential household supplies, such as cleaning and laundry supplies, towels, personal care products, toilet paper and shampoos. Don't forget to include the ones you have stockpiled. Many of them have a practical purpose, so ask yourself if you really need them now when making your decision. If you go in with the intention of fitting them all into the existing storage space in the bathroom and toilet, it will make it easier for you to determine how many things to keep and how to store them.

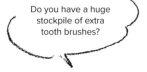

Do you have a huge stockpile of extra tooth brushes?

Gather all items in one pile and write down your observations

Example:
• The laundry bag is quite worn out
• So many tubes of prescription ointments
• Loads of pocket-size tissues

_____

_____

_____

_____

_____

_____

_____

_____

_____

_____

_____

_____

_____

Touch each one and keep only what sparks joy

Ask yourself if the fragrance, design, and/or packaging sparks joy. For practical items such as cleaning supplies and personal care products, be sure to take the functionality into consideration as well.

Give thanks to what doesn't spark joy and let it go

Give a rough estimate, e.g. 'one bin bag full', 'one box of detergent', etc.

Does the thought of using it spark joy?

If you have a hard time letting go of something just because it's still usable (a bottle of fancy detergent you received as a gift, for example), imagine yourself using it and see if that thought sparks joy. You can also donate it or sell it at a flea market.

Group what you've chosen by category

Group the household supplies by category as you imagine fitting them all into the built-in storage in the bathroom and toilet. If there's not enough room for the unused extras, move them to another location, such as a storage cupboard. Use empty boxes for organization if available, and store things upright whenever possible.

Cleaning and laundry supplies

Sort cleaning and laundry supplies by type: detergents, hangers, etc. Use baskets, boxes, magazine holders or reusable grocery bags to minimize clutter when storing them.

Hangers

Detergent

Cleaning tools

Towels

Sort towels by size, then fold them and store them upright. Since they are used every day one by one, it's okay to stack them up if you like. You can put them in a basket in the bathroom or on a shelf.

You can store them upright or stack them

Personal care items

Includes contacts, ointments, hand creams and so on. Disposable contacts and ointments look much more organized when you remove the packaging and place them upright in a small box.

Ointments and hand creams

Contact supplies

Extras

Whether it's toilet paper or shampoo, extras should generally be kept with the ones currently in use. But if there's not enough space there, group all extras as their own category. Put them inside a drawer or box and find a place for them in a cupboard or storage room.

Store extras here

Leave the bathing space empty

I make a habit to quickly wipe shampoo bottles with a used towel and put them back in their designated storage. It pays to leave the bathing space empty – it's easy to clean and you don't get any water stains!

Store the household supplies

On p.139 we sorted household supplies by category. Most of them you'd want to store in the bathroom for convenience. If you live alone, you're free to store things as you please. If you live with family, however, first decide where to keep the communal items such as the hairdryer, then divide the remaining space among the household members and store personal items accordingly. The toilet storage space can house toilet paper, female hygiene products and anything else that would only be used there.

Contacts and personal care items
Keep contacts, ointments and other small personal care items together. In the case of a multi-member household, items that are only used by a certain person can be moved to the respective individual storage spaces.

Personalized storage
In a communal space such as a bathroom, the etiquette is to respect boundaries. Assign a dedicated space for each household member to store and manage their own personal items.

Pick a place for communal items first
Reserve the most intuitive and convenient storage locations for a hairdryer, oral hygiene products and anything that's shared by the household.

Bath towels and other towels
Store towels in the bathroom drawer or the shelf above the washing machine. Stack them or keep them upright, depending on the storage space.

Detergents and shampoos in use
Group all detergents and shampoos in use together in a basket and store them under the sink. Any extras can be tucked away behind that basket for an easy inventory.

Hobby komono

Hobby komono includes tools for any lessons you take, collectibles, items for relaxation such as aromatherapy oils and special event clothes that you set aside on p.82. Each of them deserve to be stored in a way that makes them sparkle. Sorting through the collectibles can be particularly time-consuming, so be patient with yourself.

Dare to let go of past hobby supplies

Whether it's Japanese calligraphy or tea ceremony, if you come across supplies for an activity you used to take up but no longer care for, dare to let them go after giving thanks for the experience. If that's too challenging at this point, you can set them aside as sentimental items (p.171) and go through them later.

Gather all items in one pile and write down your observations

Example:
• Found Japanese calligraphy tools from back when I used to take lessons
• There's a whole box packed with collectibles

Touch each one and keep only what sparks joy

Don't assume you can't get rid of anything relating to your hobby. Go through them with fresh eyes, and you'll likely notice some of them no longer speak to your heart because your taste has shifted.

Relaxation goods themselves need to relax

Aromatherapy oils, stuffed animals and anything that promotes relaxation need to be stored in a way that allows them to relax as well. Create a calming space with baskets and partitions made of comforting natural materials to amplify the healing effect.

Give thanks to what doesn't spark joy and let it go

Give a rough estimate, e.g. 'one knitting kit', 'ski gear from twenty years ago', etc.

Store what you've chosen in an attractive manner

Hobbies are meant to enrich your life, so store the related items in a way that sparks utmost joy. Never just throw them into a box like a pile of junk! Put them on display so they're always in sight, or arrange them in a drawer or presentation book in a way that makes your heart sing every time you open it.

Storage that sparks maximum joy

Kitchen goods and food supplies

Ease of cleaning is the critical element in creating a kitchen that sparks joy. Just by clearing the sink area and keeping everything sparkling clean, you'll get better visibility of the entire kitchen and be able to work much more efficiently. To start, take out all the kitchen goods and food supplies and sort them into three subcategories as shown below. There may be a lot to go through, but the huge sense of accomplishment you'll feel once you're done will be so worth it!

Sort them into three categories and write down your observations

To tidy a wide variety of kitchen items, sort them into three general categories: eating implements (crockery and cutlery), cooking tools (pots and utensils) and food (anything that keeps at room temperature). Try to keep each category together for storage as well.

Eating implements

Example:
• The spare cutlery for guests is taking up too much room
• Dishes that were a gift are still in their boxes

Cooking tools

Example:
- The bottom of the saucepan is scorched black
- Three ladles is too many

_____
_____
_____
_____
_____
_____
_____
_____
_____
_____
_____
_____
_____

Food

Example:
- Various spices are past their expiry date
- There's a stockpile of dried food

_____
_____
_____
_____
_____
_____
_____
_____
_____
_____
_____
_____
_____

Are there any unused tools being buried?

Leave the rest for later

Set aside anything that doesn't belong to the three subcategories opposite as 'Other' to go through later on p.152: lunchboxes, cloth komono, bags, food wraps and tin foil, food storage containers, washing up tools and so on.

Touch each one and keep only what sparks joy

Although this would be a lot of work for those of you who have a lot of dishes, do the joy check on each piece one by one. This is also a chance to clean out the crockery cupboard. If you're overwhelmed by the amount and feeling indecisive, ask yourself the following questions, then let go of the things you don't think you'll be using in the future. Selling them at a flea market or online is a great idea, too.

Questions for difficult joy checks

- When was the last time I used this?
- How often do I use this?
- Do I have dishes that spark joy yet I don't use?
- Am I ignoring the dishes that are chipped or cracked?

You'll never use the boxed dishes

Do you keep dish or wine glass gift sets still in their boxes? Unless you pull them out now, you'll never use them. If they spark joy, keep them next to the everyday dishes and use them by all means.

Give thanks to what doesn't spark joy and let it go

Give a rough estimate, e.g. 'ten medium and large plates', two tea sets' etc.

Store what you've chosen in an attractive manner

Arrange the dish cupboard according to material (glass, ceramic, etc.), then divide each area into drinkware (glasses, etc.) and crockery (plates, etc.). If there's not enough surface area, adding a self-standing shelf can help.

Ceramics

Glassware

Wood

For eating

For drinking

Cutlery gets special treatment

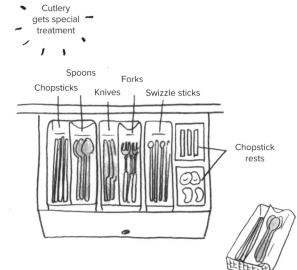

Spoons

Chopsticks

Forks

Knives

Swizzle sticks

Chopstick rests

Since cutlery is something you put directly into your mouth, give it special treatment to raise the everyday joy factor. Lay each item down luxuriously in a drawer partitioned with a cutlery tray or pieces of fabric.

Cooking tools

Touch each one and keep only what sparks joy

Joy checks for cooking tools such as pots, pans, bowls and ladles should address not only their appearance but also their design and functionality. Does it have a nice grip? Does it cut well? Something that's pleasurable to use can also be recognized as bringing you joy.

Give thanks to what doesn't spark joy and let it go

Give a rough estimate, e.g. 'one frying pan', 'two strainers' etc.

A well-used tool still qualifies as joy if it's useful

Take a wooden spatula, for example. Even if its tip has become rounded over many uses, if it fits your hand and serves you well, then there's no need to discard it. Tools you can trust deserve your certificate of joy.

Start using the extras right away

If you keep a stockpile of new and unused tools such as cooking chopsticks, this is the perfect time to swap them out with the old ones. New tools give you a fresh start when you cook, adding sparks of joy.

Store what you've chosen in an attractive manner

Cooking utensils such as ladles and spatulas can go in a utensil holder under the sink or be laid out flat in a drawer without overlapping. I usually stack pots and pans and put them in the cabinet under the sink.

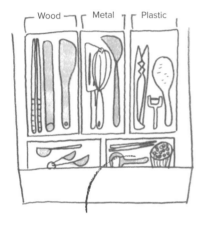

Cooking utensils

If using a drawer, create partitions to avoid clutter. Sort them according to your own categories, such as by material, and lay them flat.

Kitchen komono

Knick-knacks such as bottle openers and toothpicks can go in small compartments after you decide where to store the utensils.

Lids

Pot lids don't stack well, so for a clean storage, use organizers such as a U-shaped book stand to keep them upright.

Pots and pans

Stack items of the same shape when possible, so that you can maximize the vertical space available. You can also use a cookware rack, if available, to keep the pans upright.

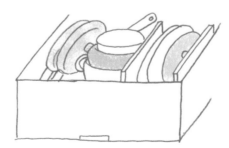

Touch each one and keep only what sparks joy

Throw away all food past its expiry date without reservation, even if it's unopened. When debating whether or not to keep an unexpired item, ask yourself: does it add joy to my cooking? Does it provide true nourishment for me and my family?

Have a cleaning out day for soon-to-expire food

If you have a lot of food whose 'use by' (or 'best by') date is fast approaching, dedicate one day to use it all up. Who knows, the unusual combination of food may inspire a new recipe! If you have leftover sake, you can pour it into the bath for silky smooth skin.

Give thanks to what doesn't spark joy and let it go

Give a rough estimate, e.g. 'ten expired food items' etc.

Store what you've chosen in an attractive manner

Categorize food into seasonings, dried food, canned food, food pouches, carbohydrates, snacks, supplements and oral medicines, etc. and store them upright whenever possible so you can easily tell how much is left. Depending on the amount, you can also sort them roughly by packaging: bags vs. boxes, for example.

Decide you'll only keep what fits in the box

Empty bagged food into matching containers for extra joy

Bagged food such as dried food and tea leaves spark way more joy when emptied out into matching canisters! Since you can see the contents at a glance, you're less likely to forget to use them as well.

Other kitchen tools and food supplies

Gather all items in one pile and write down your observations

Example:
• There's a stockpile of cling film
• So many storage containers that are getting worn out

_____

_____

_____

_____

_____

_____

_____

_____

_____

_____

_____

_____

_____

_____

_____

_____

_____

_____

_____

Touch each one and keep only what sparks joy

Discard all duplicates and any items you hardly ever use. It's the little things, like toothpicks and disposable containers, that can eventually grow into a huge stockpile. Sometimes you just need to be decisive and chuck a whole bunch of them at once.

Include your own categories of 'kitchen tools'

Whether it's a pair of flower shears or stationery for writing down recipes, you can count something as a kitchen tool if it's a necessity in your kitchen, even if it isn't directly related to cooking.

Give thanks to what doesn't spark joy and let it go

Give a rough estimate, e.g. 'two old sponges', 'three wipes', etc.

Check the fridge without removing its contents

Food in the refrigerator spoils easily, so there's no need to take it out. Look through them quickly and toss anything that's expired. As for storage, leave about 30 per cent empty for the day's leftovers and gifts, then group the existing food by category. Keep small bags of seasoning together in a container such as a plastic basket.

Store what you've chosen by category

'Other' items should also be sorted by category for storage. Start by securing storage for the three main categories (eating implements, cooking tools and food) then decide where to put the rest.

Bento and lunchbox supplies

Aside from the lunchbox itself, knick-knacks such as cupcake liners and toothpicks can easily scatter about, so keep them in small compartments inside a drawer. You can also store them in a box and put it on the corner of a shelf.

Cloth komono

Fold dish towels and rags and store them upright. Placemats may be folded, rolled or stacked depending on the design. Fold aprons and store them near other cloth komono as well.

Bags

Plastic shopping bags can be deflated, folded into a rectangle and stored upright in a small box to prevent overstocking. Keep paper bags together in one bag that's a little smaller than you'd want, so you don't accumulate these either.

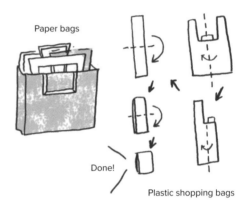

Paper bags

Done!

Plastic shopping bags

Food storage containers

This includes containers made of enamel or plastic, as well as jars and cans used for preserving food. If it's a stackable type, keep the lid and container separate; stack the containers and store the lids upright.

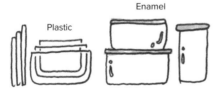

Enamel

Plastic

Cling film and tin foil

If you don't care for the package design, find a way to keep them out of sight. You can store them upright under the sink or attach a holder on the back of a cabinet door. If the holder sparks joy, however, it's okay to attach it on the outside.

Dish-washing supplies

To prevent water stains, store the detergent and sponge away from wet areas. Keep them in a basket under the sink or on the back of a cabinet door. If you use the washin up sponge all the time, however, it' okay to leave it on the sink.

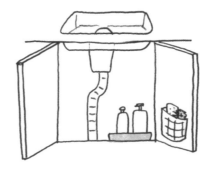

Do you have any other komono left?

Well done! Now that you've finished tidying your typical household komono, your house is likely looking much more organized. That said, everyone's lifestyle is different, and so are their komono. You probably still have things that don't belong to any of the categories we've addressed. So let's sort through them to finish.

Here I'll go over some of the more common ones, but if you come across items that fall outside of these categories, either make up a new category of your own or group them all as 'everything else', so that you leave no komono behind!

Gather the remaining komono in one spot

List the remaining komono and write down your observations

Example:
- Found a bunch of clear vinyl umbrellas
- So many souvenir keyrings

How to tidy the remaining komono

Here are several examples of miscellaneous items that my clients typically sort through after the basic komono. Let these tips on joy checks and storage help you finish tidying everything up!

Linens

When doing joy checks on linens such as sheets or pillowcases, don't just touch them – smell them. They can get mildewy if left abandoned for a long time, even if you haven't opened the packaging. So it's best to use them before that happens. Open them immediately and let them breathe.

Sniff, sniff

Leisure equipment

This is a diverse category that includes sports equipment, games and camping gear. Keep the ones that spark joy and are used at least a couple of times a year. Store them nicely in a box or bag that you love, instead of just throwing them haphazardly into a plastic shopping bag.

CAMP

Fold-out mattress for guests

Mattresses normally stored away for guests are also susceptible to mildew and dust mites. They may be available to borrow, so if you don't use them often, take this opportunity to get rid of them. As for storage, cover them with a beautiful piece of fabric and treat them with respect as you would a guest.

Did we have any overnight guests this past year?

Holiday decorations

If you have decorations for holidays such as Christmas, Halloween or Easter, keep only what you'd love to put up again the following year. Store them in garment cases or boxes organized by theme. And each time you use them, check to see if they spark joy for you now.

Christmas

Emergency preparation supplies

This is a good time for a full inspection on emergency backpacks, torches, and other supplies for emergency preparation. Check every item, then store them in a cupboard near the hallway or in the bedroom. Don't forget to discuss emergency protocols with your family as well.

Umbrellas

In theory, one umbrella per person should be plenty, yet many households have extras. Be sure to open up each one for the joy check; when left unused, the fabric can become discoloured and the metal can rust.

Charms

If you have more charms than you can carry around, create a personal altar on a surface above eye level (the top of a bookshelf, for example) and display the charms standing up so they look nice and sharp. In Japan, the custom is to take charms that are older than one year to the temple or shrine to be cremated.

Stuffed animals

This is an item that's hard to discard, even if it doesn't spark joy. Looking into the eyes of the stuffed animal can make it seem alive, so slip them into a paper bag and sprinkle a pinch of salt for purification. Thinking of this process as a memorial service makes it easier to let it go. If you still have a hard time deciding, set it aside for now as a sentimental item (p.171).

Keyrings and phone cases

People tend to keep old mobile phone cases and keyrings 'just because'. Whether it's something you bought or received as a souvenir or swag, if it doesn't spark joy, get rid of it.

Buttons

Have you ever actually sewed on an extra button you had saved just in case? Get rid of all buttons you have 'just because'. The ones that spark joy can go in the sewing box.

Keep empty boxes until you tidy sentimental items

Keep any empty boxes that pop up while tidying. You can use them to organize drawers and more. They also come in handy for making final storage adjustments at the end when you've finished tidying sentimental items (p.171).

Reflection: tidying komono

Now you've finished tidying all komono. At times you may have wondered if it'd ever end – but you did it! If you came across any items that spark joy but you don't have a purpose for, I encourage you to decorate with them, whether by placing, hanging or pinning. Try hooking a keyring onto the curtain rod or attaching a postcard or fabric you love on the back of the cupboard door. Once you're done, look around the room, take some photos and journal your thoughts and feelings before you forget.

Completed worksheet example

How was tidying komono for you?

Having tidied so many komono, your awareness towards objects must have shifted from back when you first tackled clothes. Take a note of those changes as well.

1. Describe how you feel now in a few words.

> Refreshed!

Why? The drawers and shelves used to be a huge mess, but now they're so nice and organized. It feels like I'm a new person!

2. What changes would you like to make with your komono? Example: keep the number of extras under control!

• Replace make-up with a whole new set!

• Always keep kitchen komono clean

3. What changes would you like to make in your komono storage? Example: get new boxes with a simple, cohesive design

• Make the storage under the sink and under the hob a little more functional

• Replace the open shelves with a different storage system that's easier to clean

4. What is your intention for tidying the next category (sentimental items)?

> Pick out only the best from the cardboard box full of photos and create a joy-sparking photo album!

How do you feel now that you've accomplished the monumental task of tidying so many komono? Write down the first short phrase that comes to mind.

Reflect on how you've managed komono in the past and what you'd like to do going forward, including any ideas for storage. Write them down so they become an action plan.

How was tidying komono for you?

Having tidied so many komono, your awareness towards objects must have shifted from back when you first tackled clothes. Take a note of those changes as well.

1. Describe how you feel now in a few words.

Why? _____
_____
_____
_____

2. What changes would you like to make with your komono?

Example: keep the number of extras under control!

_____
_____
_____
_____
_____
_____
_____

3. What changes would you like to make in your komono storage? Example: get new boxes with a simple, cohesive design

_____
_____
_____
_____
_____
_____
_____
_____

4. What is your intention for tidying the next category (sentimental items)?

Add your photos

Seeing your tidied room in a photo, it becomes very clear just how much transformation it went through. Compare it to the 'before' photo (p.34) and put into words what comes to mind.

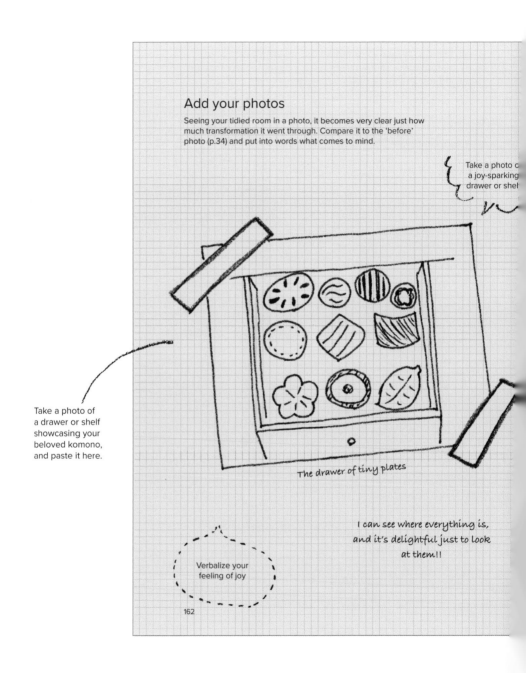

Take a photo of a joy-sparking drawer or shelf

Take a photo of a drawer or shelf showcasing your beloved komono, and paste it here.

The drawer of tiny plates

Verbalize your feeling of joy

I can see where everything is, and it's delightful just to look at them!!

162

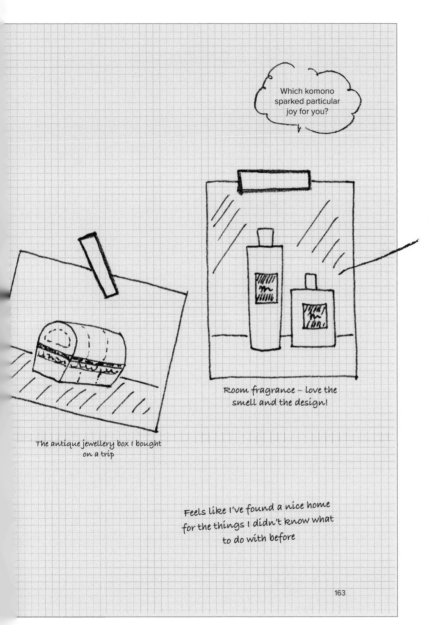

What is your absolute favourite komono that makes your heart sing? Feel free to list more than one. Photos and illustrations welcome.

Add your photos

Seeing your tidied room in a photo, it becomes very clear just how much transformation it went through. Compare it to the 'before' photo (p.34) and put into words what comes to mind.

Take a photo of a joy-sparking drawer or shelf

Verbalize your feeling of joy

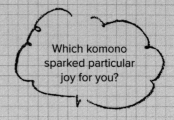

Which komono
sparked particular
joy for you?

Chapter 6

Tidy your
sentimental items

Get ready for the grand finale of your tidying campaign!

It's time to take on your sentimental items – the most challenging category to declutter because of the emotional value they carry. Rest assured, you're fully prepared for this task, having gone through clothing, books, papers and komono in the proper order. So trust your own judgement, and let the power of joy guide you in putting the past in order once and for all.

Fill in the dates when you started and finished

Started _____ (year) _____ (month) _____ (day) at _____ (time)

Finished _____ (year) _____ (month) _____ (day) at _____ (time)

How to tidy without relapsing

Although the basic protocol is to do the joy check by touch, when it comes to the final category of sentimental items, it's okay to take your time evaluating them. Have a thorough dialogue with each one, so as not to have any regrets.

1. Gather

Gather all your sentimental items from every corner of the house

Start by gathering all your sentimental items by category, including those you previously set aside while tidying clothing, books, papers or komono. Photos tend to pop up in many different places, so we'll organize them last. For now, keep them together in an empty box.

The 'joy check' order

Here is a sample order by which to sort through the sentimental items by category. It's best to start with items that are few in number and pertain only to you, so feel free to switch up the order as you see fit. Photographs likely involve other people in your life, such as family or a lover, so leave them for last, as the final step in your tidying campaign.

School memories   Memories of past lovers

2. Keep what sparks joy

When it comes to sentimental items, it's okay to take a look inside

Joy checks won't go well when you're caught up in the idea that discarding sentimental items means losing your precious memories along with them. Keep in mind that the memories are already in your heart. As for letters and records of your life, feel free to look inside and take your time making your decision.

Flip, flip

3. Store

Joy-filled sentimental items help your future shine

Keep what you've chosen with confidence, and store them in a way that allows you to look at them anytime you like, so that you can stay connected to the joy they bring. Arranging them beautifully in a dedicated drawer or hanging them on the wall are both great ideas. If you're going to store them in a box, do your best to find one that really sparks joy.

Sentimental recordings

Life records

Letters

Your children's creations

How to choose which sentimental items to keep

Trust your own ability to discern joy

The key here is to trust your own sense of joy. You've been doing countless joy checks, and it's impossible for you to make any big mistakes now. Have confidence in yourself!

Consider if your future self needs it

If you're going to keep something, you'd want to put it to good use. Be present and carefully evaluate if the sentimental item is something you need in order to make your future self shine.

It's okay to read the content of diaries and letters

Reading the content was taboo when tidying books (p.91), however, when it comes to sentimental items, feel free to read them to your heart's content. That said, don't push yourself if it's something that's emotionally challenging for you to read. Set it aside and come back to it later.

Komono that you'd set aside

The final step in your tidying campaign

Other

Photos

Tidy all your sentimental items except photos

You may be reticent to let go of the objects full of memories that once brought you joy. But you'll never lose truly precious memories even if you discard the object.

Tidying sentimental items is an act of facing the past and putting it in order. Take each one in your hands and keep only what helps your life shine in the days to come. I recommend you leave the photos for later, as it can be time-consuming, and go through all other sentimental items in one go. Approach it like you're pushing a reset button on your life – this is the grand finale of your enormous tidying campaign.

Gather all items in one pile and write down your observations

Example:
- Found my report card from elementary school
- So many cassette tapes
- Lots of embarrassing diaries

_____

_____

_____

_____

_____

_____

_____

Touch each one and keep only what sparks joy

We live in the present, not in the past. So what really matters is not the glory of the past that an item represents but whether it brings you happiness now. Take your time and have a dialogue with your own heart.

Give thanks to what doesn't spark joy and let it go

Give a rough estimate, e.g. 'Two bin bags full', etc.

How to tidy sentimental items

Here are some tips for checking, discarding and storing various types of sentimental items. The question to keep in mind throughout is whether it's something you really need going forward.

School memories

Try to save space by keeping only one noteworthy report card, consolidating all diplomas into one scroll holder, displaying only the most meaningful trophies, and so on. If you have trouble parting with an old school uniform, try it on. Indulge yourself in the memories and do your joy check in front of the mirror. My clients often snap to their senses after doing this and end up letting it go without any difficulty.

'NG' = no good, don't do this

Never ship things off to your parents' house!

Just because there's room at your parents' house, it doesn't mean you're allowed to send them a container full of sentimental items. That box would never be opened; you'd just be trying to avoid confronting the past.

Memories of past lovers

If you want to attract new relationships, I recommend that you get rid of all memories of past lovers. That said, it's fine to keep using a gifted accessory or bag that has become your go-to, as long as it doesn't trigger any memories. When discarding, add a pinch of salt for purification and express gratitude.

Sentimental recordings

You may have recordings of a trip or wedding saved on CDs, DVDs or Blu-ray discs. If you're not sure of the content, play just the beginning as needed to determine if it's worth keeping. If you have cassette tapes or VHS tapes that spark joy but no longer have a player, you might like to use a transfer service. Be sure to place the order immediately instead of putting it off for later.

Your children's creations

If you can't bring yourself to discard the things that your children made for you, why not think of ways to take good care of them? You can designate a specific corner for displaying them or put them in a special box for you to look through every once in a while. Sometimes the opportunity to let go of something arrives after taking enough time to appreciate it.

Life records

One approach to diaries and date books is to flip through the pages and choose one from the most joyful year to keep. Feel free to keep maternal and child handbooks if they still spark joy. If you want to keep ticket stubs from a trip, put them in a scrapbook so that you can enjoy them at any time.

Letters

Look over each letter one by one. When discarding, place the letter in an opaque bag before throwing it into the rubbish. If rereading the letter brings you comfort or encouragement and you decide to keep it, put it in a box and save it somewhere away from moisture so that it doesn't deteriorate.

Update your growing collection of sentimental items every now and then

Although you'll be acquiring more sentimental items in the future, taking the time to fully appreciate them can help you feel good about letting them go. As for purely sentimental items that you can't use in your everyday life, keep them together in a special box. Look over them every once in a while and keep only what sparks joy in the now moment.

Other

This is the time to do your joy check on items you previously set aside while tidying clothes or komono. You may be surprised at how dispassionately and smoothly you can make the decision to let things go now. If you decide something does spark joy after all, make a commitment to use it well and appreciate it.

How was tidying sentimental items (besides photos) for you?

With the exception of photos, you've now successfully tidied your sentimental items. Before you forget, write down how you feel and what you've learned by confronting your past.

1. Describe how you feel now in a few words.

Why? _____
_____
_____
_____

2. What changes would you like to make with your sentimental items? Example: let's go see the sentimental items buried in my parents' house!

_____
_____
_____
_____
_____
_____

3. What changes would you like to make in your sentimental items storage? Example: I want a pretty box to put letters in

_____
_____
_____
_____
_____
_____

4. How have you changed since you started tidying?

Tidy photos as the final step in your tidying campaign

Organizing photos is the last and final step – not only in the sentimental items category but also your entire tidying campaign.

Sorting through a massive collection of photo prints that represent your personal history is a task that you should only undertake when you've developed sufficient judgement. Otherwise, you're bound to get stuck half way, and things can spiral out of control. But I know for certain that you've honed your sensitivity to joy quite a bit by now. So proceed with confidence.

In general you'll be taking the photos in your hand one by one, but if you already have a photo album that sparks joy as a whole, it's fine to keep it as is.

If a photo album sparks joy, leave it as is

Gather all items in one pile and write down your observations

Example:
- There are a lot of photos that look similar
- Found a huge pile of old negatives
- One of the albums had become discoloured

_____

_____

_____

_____

_____

_____

_____

_____

_____

_____

_____

_____

_____

_____

_____

_____

_____

_____

_____

Look at each one and keep only what sparks joy

The rule of thumb is to discard all old negatives. Throw away unmemorable landscape photos, and if you come across multiple photos with a similar composition, select the best one. As you make your photo selections, my recommendation is to lay them out on the floor according to year they were taken. It's a fun way to visually organize your history.

Tidy family photos with your family

Tidying family photos with your family is a great idea. It's really fun to pick out the photos together while reminiscing about good times. The photos that you end up selecting and keeping in this way are sure to become family treasures.

New – Old

Same year

Give thanks to what doesn't spark joy and let it go

Give a rough estimate, e.g. 'one cardboard box full', '20 pocket-size albums', etc.

Store what you've chosen in an attractive manner

Once you've organized the selected photos by year, put them all together in an 'album of joy'. For the photos that you particularly love, you may choose to decorate your room with them instead. The trick to fully appreciating your memories is to make sure you can enjoy them at any time.

Don't just keep photos in a box

Now that you've taken the time and energy to organize the photos, it would be a waste to just keep them in a box, because it substantially lowers the chance that you'd look through them. Putting them together in an album is a must, so that you can casually review them anytime you want.

Discard photos in a paper bag or envelope

Photos of people can be hard to throw away because you feel like their eyes are watching you. If you have two or more, stack them with the pictures facing inwards and slip them into an opaque paper bag or envelope before discarding them. If you want to clear away any karma with the person in the photo, add in a pinch of purification salt.

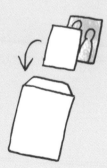

How was tidying photos for you?

Now that you've organized so many photos, what emotions are coming up? It's important to reflect on your honest feelings and to set intentions for the future here.

1. Describe how you feel now in a few words.

Why? _____

_____

_____

_____

_____

_____

_____

_____

_____

_____

2. What changes would you like to make in organizing and storing your photos? Example: Go buy a photo album that I love ASAP!

_____

_____

_____

_____

_____

_____

_____

_____

_____

_____

_____

_____

_____

_____

_____

_____

_____

_____

The objects you've chosen out of joy are longing to serve you

From clothing to books, papers, komono and sentimental items – you've now completed your entire tidying campaign with joy as your guide. Right now, you are in a room filled only with the things you love and have chosen to keep. As you go about your daily life alongside these beloved items, I'd like to ask you a favour: please make it a practice to show them appreciation. When you come home, say 'Thank you for carrying me through another day' to your shoes as you remove them, 'Thank you for keeping me warm for another day' to your clothes as you take them off, and 'Thank you for protecting my belongings for another day' to your bag as you place it down. Take a moment to thank the objects for supporting you throughout the day, and speak kindly to them as you put them back in their designated spot. I believe showing a little appreciation goes a long way, even if you don't do it every single day.

Each object that found its way to your home is a unique, one-of-a-kind entity. And your relationships with objects are just as valuable and meaningful as your relationships with people. Every item you've chosen to keep is longing to serve you. Even if you were to throw them away, the energetic imprint of their desire to serve will remain – and each will eventually find its way back to you as another object that brings you joy. All the many objects you let go of this time around are eager to make their way back to you in another form.

Fully use the objects you love in your daily life

• Use them as often as possible
• Use them with care
• Give thanks and show appreciation

Objects come to life when you use them. The purpose of your favourite teacup is not to be tucked away in the cabinet. When you use it, you'll naturally handle it with care and pour tea into it with an elegant and mindful gesture. And that cup of tea will taste so delicious that you'd feel gratitude welling up from within. It's by making full use of the things you love that you invite happy times into your life.

With tidying complete, your life will change dramatically

Now that you've finished tidying and assigned a home to every single object in the house, all you need to do going forward is return things to where they belong each time you use them. With no homeless objects to create clutter, your room will always be tidy. And since you know where everything is, you'll no longer spend time and energy looking for what you need. A greater sense of ease will permeate your day-to-day life. The days of feeling overwhelmed by tidying are over.

There's no doubt that tidying changes your life. As you go through the process of touching each object and repeatedly asking yourself if it sparks joy, you'll gradually feel more confident in your own discernment and start to build self-esteem. When you know what you love and what brings you joy, it becomes clear what you really want to do. And now you can enjoy your own life wholeheartedly. One of my clients had a business opportunity fall into their lap as soon as they got rid of a huge pile of old business cards. Another client remembered their true passion and switched careers after tidying their book collection.

These are just a few examples of the countless testimonials by people whose lives were completely transformed by tidying.

So what truly sparks joy for you, now that your tidying festival has come to a close? This is where your real life begins. I hope that going forward, you will pour as much of your time and passion as you can into what brings you joy.

The two changes after tidying

The only tidying you need to do is to put things back where they belong
= Daily tasks become easier

Grow confident in your own judgement
= Increased self-esteem

How did your tidying campaign go?

Great job! All tidying is now complete. Add a photo of your tidy room and journal your current feelings as well as thoughts for the future.

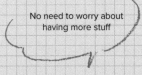

No need to worry about having more stuff

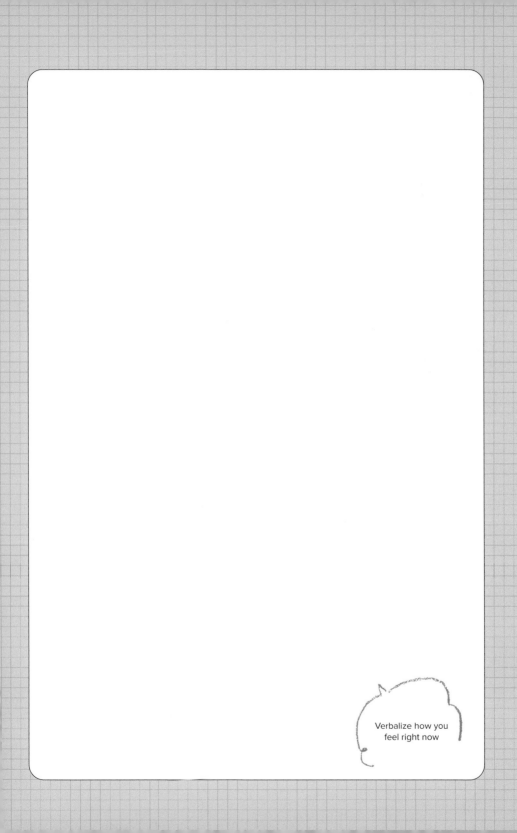

Verbalize how you
feel right now

Conclusion

Well done on your tidying festival!

How was your experience of putting the KonMari Method into practice? Now that you're surrounded by the things you love, you may be feeling lighter than ever, enjoying a sense of comfort as if you're being protected by a higher power.

Some of you, however, may be worried about accumulating things and relapsing to clutter, or feeling frustrated by a storage issue you haven't fully resolved yet.

But that doesn't mean you need to live by strict rules, such as 'If I buy something, I have to let something else go'. It's better to naturally hone your sensitivity to joy through your day-to-day interaction with the objects around you.

The key is to always be grateful for what you have. And to find the small things in your daily life that bring you joy, so that you can spend more and more of your time feeling happy.

It can be as trivial as opening the window and feeling a nice breeze or feeling good about cleaning the kitchen until it's spick-and-span just before going to bed. Start by appreciating the little sparks of joy throughout the day. Gradually, you will develop a greater ability to sense joy. You will begin to naturally notice if a bag doesn't actually spark joy or a sweater is just about ready to retire from its service. All you need to do is let things go when that happens.

Once you've finished your tidying festival, there's no need for another full-blown festival per se. But I highly recommend having a 'mini tidying festival' whenever you go through a significant event in your life.

I myself let go of several things and readjusted storage locations before welcoming my child. By reviewing our possessions at each stage of our lives, we become aware of our current state of mind. This gives us the clarity we need to set our course of action in preparation for the next phase.

If you've succeeded in downsizing but are anxious to get storage right, you may want to ask for professional help instead of continuing to struggle on your own. There are many tidying professionals in Japan, so why not consider booking a private lesson with one of them?

May your life continue to spark more and more joy!

KonMari (Marie Kondo)

Notes

Notes

Notes

Notes

Notes

Notes

Notes